p 94 Which practice right for me? p3
If suffering come
pg 97, puja? W
gratitude to L
dedicate life to gratit
present each moment   (fellow)
p 100 - Samana Sanna = Seekers of
peace - focus on our similarity
to support our own practice

Beginning Our Day

Volume One

p 102 our collective going forth = commitmt
raised up, lifted = from confusion + self centered
to being mindful, awake.

Dhamma Reflections from Abhayagiri Monastery

our changing Bodies 104

Part of Picture 106

p 108 - Community life vs solitude,
(birth, death). When I help others it
lessons my self-centredness
and my unhealthy sense of
self-importance

p 110 caring for everything we use
stuff - using mindfully.
p 112 Reflect on Inter dependence
Let go of ignorant qualities: greed,
Self interest,   selfishness,
Cultivate virtue   and generosity.
p 115 Rock Climbing = meditation?
= discerning awareness focus on
suffering or dis-ease Questions: Cause?
Resolution? How I bring about
resolution

[Handwritten notes at top of page:]

P117, Mindfulness, moods, defilements
OBSERVE: thoughts, moods passing
by = clouds across the sky.
defilement = desire, observe
ask for help. It will not go away
on its own (MacBeth's wife)
Mind - attended p 119
= my JOB, my responsibility. I gotta
do it - I'm the only one being
responsible. Mind creates
significance = its not
center of world,
gravity works
on its own.

Abhayagiri Buddhist Monastery
16201 Tomki Road
Redwood Valley, California 95470
www.abhayagiri.org
707-485-1630

Interior design by Suhajjo Bhikkhu. Cover design by Sumi Shin.
Cover photos by Jonathan Payne.

We would like to acknowledge the support of the Kataññutā group of
Malaysia, Singapore, and Australia for bringing this book into full
production.

[Handwritten notes:]

p122 - Superior Resolve
Notice your atten
when you are about
your actions
Pay atten to the result
the resolve has on our activity

FSC
MIX
FSC™ C084469

Printed using paper from a sustainable source.

sabbadānaṃ dhammadānaṃ jināti.

The gift of Dhamma excels all gifts.

p 124 Dissolving practice

Let go of control, self-image,

self-territories.

Perfectionism? ∴ → dissolving p. 124

p 127

This book is dedicated to our teachers and parents.

Contents

Preface

"Beginning our day . . ."

These quintessential words are spoken by Luang Por Pasanno before he begins each of his morning reflections.

Five days a week, at Abhayagiri's morning meeting, work tasks are assigned to the residents and guests living in the monastery. Shortly thereafter, one of the senior monks offers a brief Dhamma reflection so that the residents and guests have something meaningful to recollect throughout their day.

These talks are given spontaneously and often address an event that is about to occur, a condition that is already present in the monastery, or a general teaching on Dhamma. The most common thread through all the reflections is that of practicality: distilling the most important teachings of the Buddha into pertinent and applicable practices. Though many different teachings are touched upon, the fundamental aim is to encourage the abandonment of the unwholesome, the cultivation of the wholesome, and the purification of the mind.

While several of these teachings may be read together at one time, readers might find it more useful to focus on a single reflection so they can easily recollect, contemplate, and make use of it throughout their day.

This book was made possible through the contributions of many people. More than ten years ago, Pamela Kirby initiated the project when she placed a recorder in front of one of the senior monks during a morning reflection and proposed that a book be written. Matthew Grad, Jeff Miller, Ila

Lewis, Ray Peterson, and Laurent Palmatier were the main substantive editors of the material, enduring the long and difficult process of editing the transcripts into compact and well-written teachings. Pamela Kirby generously offered assistance at various stages of the editing process. Ruby Grad helped with the copy editing. Shirley Johannesen helped with the glossary. David Burrowes, Dee Cope, Josh Himmelfarb, Evan Hirsch, Jeanie Daskais, Anagārika John Nishinaga, and members of the Lotus Volunteer Group: Wendy Parker and Viveka all helped with further refining of the text. Sumi Shin designed the cover. Jonathan Payne took the cover photos. Michael Smith tumbled the stones for the back cover.

For several years, Khemako Bhikkhu recorded the senior monks' reflections. Kovilo Bhikkhu and Pesalo Bhikkhu provided corrections on an early draft of the book. Suhajjo Bhikkhu generously dedicated a significant amount of time on the overall book design and typesetting of the text.

The Collected Teachings of Ajahn Chah published by Aruna Publications in 2011 provided many of the terms in the glossary.

The Kataññutā group of Malaysia, Singapore, and Australia generously brought this book into full production.

Any errors that remain in these reflections are my own responsibility.

May these teachings bring insight into the nature of Dhamma and provide a pathway toward the development of true peace and contentment.

Cunda Bhikkhu
Abhayagiri Monastery
May 2014

Abbreviations

DN	Dīgha Nikāya
MN	Majjhima Nikāya
SN	Saṃyutta Nikāya
AN	Aṅguttara Nikāya
Sn	Sutta Nipāta
Cp	Cariyāpiṭaka
Jā	Jātaka

Directing Attention Skillfully

Luang Por Pasanno • April 2005

Learning how to meditate—how to develop the mind—is learning how to direct attention in a skillful way. Whatever we direct our attention toward becomes our reality. If we like, we can direct attention to all the chaos in the world or to the chaos of our own personal dramas. But we don't have to do that. We can instead direct our minds to contemplate our experiences as merely form, feeling, perception, mental formations, and consciousness. We can direct our attention in other skillful ways as well—toward objects that soothe the mind and conduce to peace and clarity. It's simple: We can incline the mind toward what is wholesome or what is troublesome. The choice we make is up to each one of us.

Santuṭṭhi and the
Meaning of Contentment

Ajahn Amaro • December 2008

Contentment, or *santuṭṭhi*, is often talked about in the context of material possessions, particularly in our reflections on the four requisites of robes, alms food, lodging, and medicine. It's the quality of being content with whatever is offered—the food that's presented to us each day, whatever shelter is available to us for one night, and whatever robes and medicine are accessible to us. That's an important aspect of contentment and a very grounding one—to have few material needs and few material possessions. There's a story about a man who found every one of his possessions torched in a large bonfire. All that remained were some ashes and the buckles from his boots. His response was, "Well, good, now I don't have to bother with all that stuff anymore." This is what it means to be content with what we have—doing without if need be or living in our dwelling places with the thought that it is only a roof over our head for one night. This is our training.

It's also important to consider how santuṭṭhi permeates all aspects of the path. It's not solely a matter of renunciation or not being moved by desire, agitation, or fear in terms of material things or how we relate to other people. Contentment is also the basis for concentration, *samādhi*—that quality of being content with this moment, this breath, this footstep, this feeling in the knee, this sound in the room, this quality of mood. To be content with just this moment is of enormous importance in terms of samādhi, concentration. And if there's discontent—*I have to become more concentrated, gain more insight, be more comfortable, I have to, I have to*—then even though we may be well intentioned, discontent continually creates a cause for agitation and a lack of focus. As a result, samādhi is far away.

The quality of contentment can drift off in certain ways. It can turn into dullness or laziness or an urge to switch off, while at the same time we're thinking of ourselves as being content. Actually, we're simply steering the mind toward numbness, a non-feeling state or a feeling of wanting to get rid of, not bothering with. That's not contentment. Contentment isn't a quality of begrudging resignation—*Oh well, I'm stuck with this mood, this particular problem or feeling. I'll just grit my teeth and bear it. I'll just wait for this to be over*—this is merely dullness, a nihilistic attitude. By contrast, when we are content there is a bright, radiant quality present. Contentment has a great lightness and clarity to it.

Contentment can also drift off in the opposite direction into complacency, self-satisfaction, being pleased with ourselves. *I'm fine. I don't need to do anything with my mind. Everything is perfect.* That's taking it too far in the opposite direction. Contentment is a bright and energetic state, but it's also free from self view and self-centeredness. It's not colored by an I-me-mine attitude.

Santuṭṭhi is not only a basis for samādhi, but also for *vipassanā*, insight. It's the ability to be content with seeing this feeling, this thought, this mood, or this memory as a pattern of nature. We're not buying into it, trying to read a story into

3

it, or claiming it as self or other. Contentment allows us to leave things alone. A painful memory arises, does its thing, and ceases. An exciting fantasy arises, does its thing, and ceases. An important responsibility arises, does its thing, and ceases. That's it. This is a characteristic of contentment, we're able to leave things alone. The mental formations, the patterns of the world—we can let them be. It's not because we're switching off, we don't care, or we're resentfully resigned to some situation. Rather, it's a gentleness and presence of mind, a sense of the fullness of being. We're not needing to extract something from this thought, this feeling, this moment, or this experience.

Vipassanā is based on being able to attend simply to the process of an experience, rather than buying into its content. This requires restraint and in particular, sense restraint: not maneuvering to get more in the way of our requisites, not getting fussy and picky in terms of robes, food, shelter, or medicine. It's very basic. But the things we learn on such a basic, material level reach right to the core of our training, our spiritual practices, and our development of insight. It's the same with the quality of contentment—being at ease, tapping into the fullness of Dhamma, the completeness of Dhamma. It's always here because contentment is related to the quality of wholeness. It reflects the wholeness and the completeness of Dhamma. Nothing is missing, nothing needs to be added or taken away. Knowing this, we can be content with the way things are.

Breaking the Momentum

Ajahn Yatiko • April 2013

We can take these next few minutes as a time to establish mindfulness and provide ourselves with a break. We can break the momentum of the mind, which so easily gets caught up in the process of becoming, especially when we have ongoing projects and duties to attend to. It can be so easy for the mind to obsess about unfinished tasks, keeping itself in a chaotic world. If we find ourselves stuck thinking about a project incessantly—trying to get it organized, straight, and complete—we can take a few minutes to stop.

If we can't stop that momentum, at least we can look to see if we have the mindfulness to recognize the flow of thoughts that come with it. We can pay careful attention to the mind that is creating time, a future, plans, and everything else and try to recognize and contemplate how this process is manifesting in our present moment experience. This is a very useful form of mindfulness, and we may find it to be a very valuable reflection when this momentum of becoming is such that we can't seem to stop it.

When we're not able to step outside of our usual patterns of thinking and instead find ourselves caught up in the flow of becoming or in the momentum of any kind of pattern—and we're identified with it—then it is similar to a form of craziness. Luang Por Chah famously once said that three seconds without mindfulness is like three seconds of madness. So even though we are wearing robes or are dedicated lay practitioners, we can still share the exact same chaotic mental state as 99 percent of the rest of the planet. In those instances we are caught up in the same momentum and are identified with it, not questioning it, and flowing on and on in the stream of becoming. So we need to use these opportunities and formal structures like meetings, *pūjās*, Dhamma talks, and reflections to break that pattern. For you laypeople living outside of a monastery it is important to encourage yourselves to find environments where you can create a break in that flow of momentum. This can provide a space to establish mindfulness and allow you to reflect on your life skillfully. Otherwise life ends up being determined by patterns that have already been set in motion in the past—you're simply riding a wave. It may be difficult to find such places for yourselves, but it is important that you try.

These morning reflections are not just something to bear with and get over so we can get on to our jobs; they're here for us to use, to take up as subjects for contemplation. If we don't see very clearly how to use them in a skillful way, then we need to take that on as a reflection in and of itself. We can spend some time on the walking path or while we are sitting and ask ourselves, *What is the morning reflection for? What is the right attitude to have when it is given?* Based on what arises out of this questioning, we can challenge ourselves further and ask, *If this is the right attitude, is it something that I manage to have and cultivate, or have I allowed myself to have gotten into the habit of resisting formal structures?*

We are giving ourselves the space and time to pay attention to this flow of becoming and to use these reflections and wholesome structures to break the mind's unwholesome habits. By doing that we are slowing down the momentum of being re-lentlessly caught in cycles of rebirth and suffering. And when we have learned how to uproot this cycle, we come to a natural place of peace and freedom.

Examining
Uncomfortable Experiences

Luang Por Pasanno • June 2013

Two days ago it was the anniversary of Ajahn Chah's birth. Many aspects of his life are well worth recalling and reflecting upon. Certainly one of them is the practical approach he used to teach and encourage us. He always emphasized the importance of reflecting on the Four Noble Truths and the experience of *dukkha*—suffering, dis-ease, discontent—and the different ways we create dukkha within the heart. In this, Ajahn Chah embodied the quality of fearlessness—he had no fear when looking at the uncomfortable aspects of his own experience. By contrast, there is a tendency many of us have to try and run away from the uncomfortable experiences in our lives, to gloss them over or put some kind of spin on them. Instead, we need to look at them closely, without feeling intimidated.

I remember an example Ajahn Chah gave about this. He said, "Sometimes you get a splinter in your foot. It's kind of small, and you don't feel it all the time, but every once in a while you step in a particular way that causes you to be irritated by it. So the thought arises, *I really have to do something about this splinter.* Then you carry on and forget about it. But the irritation keeps returning until at one point you say to yourself, *I really need to do something about this splinter now. It's not something*

8

I can put up with anymore. Finally you dig it out. The experience of dukkha is the same."

It's not as if we're experiencing dukkha all the time; for the most part, we live incredibly comfortable lives here. But there's this recurring sense of dis-ease, discontent, dissatisfaction. We need to make a strong determination to investigate it, understand it, resolve it, relinquish it, not shrink back from it, and really try to dig it out. We are trying to understand the nature of the human condition—the condition that keeps us cycling back to that feeling of dis-ease. It's a willingness to patiently put forth effort and to work with our experiences. This is an opportunity for us to learn how to do that in our daily lives and to learn how to do that in our formal meditation. It's possible to be carrying that investigation with us at all times.

Mindful of Right Effort

Ajahn Karuṇadhammo • November 2012

Both on and off the cushion, we can examine how the activity of daily life is brought into the practice of Dhamma. In terms of the Noble Eightfold Path, many path factors are concerned with activities off the cushion. Developing *samādhi* with sitting is just one part of the path. There is so much more that one needs to do to practice well and correctly. If we think of practice as that which is only on the cushion, then we are going to miss almost all the opportunities in our lives for deepening the practice.

We should keep in mind throughout the day not only right mindfulness but right effort. We do this by tapping into the awareness of wholesome or unwholesome states presently occurring in the mind.

It is important to check in with our current mind states, periodically investigating the mood of the mind so that appropriate attention is paid to what is happening. We can ask ourselves if we are dwelling in an unhelpful hindrance of aversion, craving, or some sense of impatience. Do we try to rush and finish an activity so that we can be by ourselves or do something that is more interesting than what we are involved in right now? If there is a hindrance present, notice what that state of mind feels like.

If they are unwholesome mind states or states that take us to a place that is going to lead to more stress and suffering for

10

us or other people, then we can switch our attention and move into a state that will have a more positive effect on the mind. We don't need to reinforce negative states and allow them to drag us down.

Or conversely, is what we are experiencing wholesome or something that is helpful to support in the mind? We might, for example, enjoy being part of a work team and have positive experiences with other people. Or we might work alone and enjoy a wholesome activity that's good for the monastery. We can notice and reflect on these wholesome states of mind, encouraging, supporting, developing, and maintaining them.

Our goal throughout the day then, both on and off the cushion, is to check in every now and again as to the mood and quality of the mind. From there, we adjust as needed to bring about the wholesome and decrease the unwholesome.

CIA crav, impatience, aversion

A Balanced Perspective

Luang Por Pasanno • April 2013

As most of us know, when bringing the practice into our daily lives, it's necessary to apply mindfulness. But it's also necessary to ensure that our mindfulness is operating under an appropriate and beneficial view or perspective. If we are mindful, but our view is misguided, then it's likely that we're mindfully following some sort of bias or obsession.

In order to keep on the right track, we need to question the views we superimpose on our experience. One way to expose those views is to notice the way we react to experience with comments and assumptions such as, *This is really good—I like this. This is awful—I don't like this.* Reactions like those are habitual and need to be questioned.

When the mind assumes it likes an experience, it tends to block out the negative aspects in order to prop up the view, *I like this.* So we need to deliberately bring up the negative side for examination, asking ourselves, *What are the drawbacks? What are the pitfalls in this? How might I get hooked by it?* In the same way, when the mind experiences something it assumes is undesirable or challenging, we need to look at the situation from another perspective and ask ourselves, *What's the beneficial side of this experience? What can I learn from it?*

When we examine our experience from both sides in this way, it makes us more flexible with regard to the views we hold. Instead of habitually seeing things as all black or white, we can open to a more balanced perspective from which we can see that experience is never just black or white—it's always a mixture. Without this balanced perspective, we tend to go through cycles of elation and depression, excitement and frustration and then wonder why that's happening. Well, in all likelihood, it's happening because we've attached ourselves to some sort of all-or-nothing view.

Ajahn Chah encouraged us to question our views of experience by having us ask ourselves, *Is this for sure? Is this really what's happening?* By doing that, we can better adapt to whatever circumstance we find ourselves in, because we're no longer preoccupied with trying desperately to force circumstances to be the way we like them. And it becomes easier to be mindful and present with experience as it unfolds.

So whether we're attending to our duties, engaged in some kind of interaction, or alone, we need to question the habitual views and reactions that come up for us. Otherwise, those views and reactions will toss us around like a feather in the wind— wherever the wind blows, that's where we'll land.

Don't Fill Up the Void

Ajahn Jotipālo • July 2012

Why did you come to Abhayagiri? What brought you here? Simply bring that inquiry into your mind.

After traveling for the last month and being fairly busy, I returned to Abhayagiri a few days ago. I've tended to go back to my *kuṭi* in the afternoons, and it's been really quiet. There have been no expectations or demands on me. I've noticed in the past, after a period of busyness, when I go back to my kuṭi for some quiet time, there is a feeling of melancholy that comes up and a feeling that I should be doing something. I've been looking at that for the last two days, going back to my kuṭi and sitting there with that feeling. I'm not trying to label it—anxiety, depression, or whatever else the mind wants to call it. I'm just looking at it as a physical sensation and seeing how the mind is reacting to it, how the mind is trying to figure out what it is, and why it's there. When I feel this way my tendency and desire is to say to myself, *I should go do something to help the monastery or read a book or do walking meditation* ... There is this low-grade desire in me to avoid feeling this melancholy. I don't *want* to feel it. Even something as wholesome as reading or studying, if the intention behind that is to avoid feeling something, then it's good to investigate that.

For at least a period of our afternoon, when we have solitude, I think it is good to set aside some time to do nothing in particular. Don't think of it as trying to meditate or trying to focus on the mind, just sit there and be willing to feel what you're feeling. See what happens. See if it's aversion or pleasure. To me, this really gets back to that first question, *What brought me here?* We are often trying to fill up the void we feel with activities, planning, or whatever, merely because we don't want to feel the discomfort of that void, or of any other unwanted emotion. When we do this, we are not honoring the wholesome intentions that brought us here. So instead, when we find ourselves avoiding our experience, we can take the time to be quiet and be willing to feel what we are feeling.

Stopping

Luang Por Pasanno • July 2005

The other night Ajahn Sucitto gave a Dhamma talk about the type of kamma that leads to the end of kamma, and one type of kamma he spoke about was stopping. The importance of stopping is often overlooked. We get so caught up in doing, becoming, activity, and engagement that we don't attend to stopping—it's a neglected aspect of our practice. This isn't about sitting around doing nothing, because that's a form of doing as well. It's about stopping habits of greed, irritation, and confusion. It's about stepping back and ceasing.

Throughout the day, during work periods and in meditation, we can reflect on how much the mind gets swept up in activity and in identifying with that activity. We can also reflect on how this tendency moves the mind toward restlessness and agitation from which we lose our center: one little push, the ball starts rolling, and pretty soon we've worked ourselves into a state of anger and conflict. With desire, it often starts with the merest sort of interest, which then becomes liking, fascination ... and then we begin to lose control. We don't know how to stop this momentum of desire because we're not used to stopping. It's also helpful to reflect on the occasions when we do happen to stop. We might ask ourselves, *Does stopping mean I can't function? Or is it more that when I stop and stand in awareness, I accomplish things more skillfully than when the mind is swept up by moods and thoughts?*

These reflections help motivate us to learn how to stop the mind, how to stop the flow of proliferating thoughts and moods that draw us into attraction or aversion. If we learn how to stop the mind and exercise that skill frequently, then even in challenging circumstances, we will be able to bring things to a point of stillness inside and return to a clear center of awareness.

So how do we learn to stop? When we feel the mind moving and proliferating, how do we stop and come back to a place of awareness where we can attend to what the mind is doing and is intending to do? To begin, we can recognize when the mind has stopped on its own. Then we can observe what stopping itself feels like—the actual *experience* of ceasing to engage with mental activity and mental impulses. Once we become familiar with how stopping feels, we'll know when our conscious efforts to cultivate stopping are on the right track. It's helpful to make this cultivation into a regular exercise—something to frequently work, play, and experiment with.

Certainly we need to engage in activities and attend to our duties and responsibilities, but we can bring an attitude of stopping into the midst of this activity, whether it's the stopping of obsession, worry, fear, competition, aversion, or whatever. We may try to replace such unwelcome mind states with something we feel is more appropriate for "good Buddhists," but trying to replace one thing with another is yet another form of doing. Instead, if we simply attend to stopping, we learn to trust in fundamental clarity and wisdom.

Loving-Kindness for Ourselves

Ajahn Yatiko • December 2012

When we do *mettā* meditation, loving-kindness meditation, it's often good to start with ourselves. But when doing that, it is important that we not put ourselves under our thumbs—making demands about who we are and what we should be. When this happens, it's as if we're looking at the mind the way judgmental parents look at their child, power tripping and demanding that the child behave in a particular way. *I'm going to tell this kid what to do, and he's going to do what I say!* There can be no joy in approaching the mind with the assumption that it will toe the line if we force it to do so. Joy has to be unfettered with a sense of real freedom.

When we practice loving-kindness meditation, we turn our awareness and consciousness toward our sense of being, our sense of existence, and we give ourselves the space and freedom to be exactly as we are. There are no demands placed on us—not on our physical bodies or on our personalities. All of our expectations are irrelevant; they are a fiction. We give ourselves freedom to be what we are, and from that freedom we wish for ourselves, *May I be happy.*

For many of us, there can sometimes be a sense or even an insight that our *modus operandi* is not to be happy. For me, when I look at my own behavior, it doesn't always feel like it's coming from a wish for happiness. It can be like that for all of us, so we cultivate mettā as an antidote. We turn our awareness

18

toward mettā, and eventually we may have a deeper insight: *Actually, I really do want to be happy, and my heart genuinely wants that freedom.* The greatest freedom we can experience is not the freedom of letting ourselves do what we want out in the world. The Buddha says that freedom in its highest form is freedom from affliction; it's not from the gratification of the senses. It's simply the experience of sitting here with very little suffering occurring for us; we're not making problems out of our experience.

When we have loving-kindness for ourselves, we want to imbibe the sense that we are what we are, and we don't need to make a problem out of any of it. We want to tune into the sense that generating loving-kindness for ourselves *is* what our hearts want—we want to be happy and free from suffering. We genuinely want to care for ourselves. It's almost insane how we don't act in our own best interests, how we forget that this is actually what we need to be doing. So we need to make a conscious effort to value our own well-being and to recognize the heartfelt wish for our own happiness.

When doing loving-kindness meditation, we give ourselves space, freedom, and acceptance. We express ourselves from a nonjudgmental attitude, *I am what I am, and however I am, that's okay.* We bring up the wish, *May I be happy.* Then we relax into that space and see what happens.

To See the True Nature of Things

Luang Por Pasanno • December 2004

Without clearly understanding the processes of our minds, we create all kinds of problems. We are dragged about by emotional states. For there to be personal and global peace, these states need to be understood. The ways of the mind need to be seen clearly. This is the function and value of Dhamma.

When we are feeling enthusiastic, we can easily give ourselves to the practice. But it can also happen that, at times, we feel completely disillusioned, even to the extent that we forget the original confidence and faith we had. But that's natural. It's like swimming a long way. We become tired. There's no need to panic, we can simply be still for a while. Then when we have regained strength, we continue. When we understand in accordance with nature, we understand these states will change. Despair, if that is what has arisen, will pass. We keep practicing. By observing our minds and seeing how our attitudes are continually changing, we more clearly understand that impermanence is natural.

Isn't cultivating Dhamma as important as breathing? If we stop breathing, then we die. If we are not established in the right understanding of truth—the truth of the way things are— then also we die. We lose touch with what is truly good. If we are lacking the richness of truth in our hearts, then when we die and they cremate us, our lives will be worth no more than the handful of ashes we produce—and that's not much! We must investigate how to live in a way that truly accords with what the Buddha taught. Then we can live in harmony without conflicts, difficulties, and problems. *Sīla*, morality, is that which shows us the Buddha's Middle Way. It points to the avoidance of the extremes of pleasure and pain; it means knowing the right amount. When we live in the Middle Way regarding actions of body and speech, then we don't cause offense to others; we do what is appropriate for human beings. The practice of formal meditation is to train our minds and hearts to stay in the Middle Way.

Many people who meditate try to force their minds to be as they want them to be. They sit there arguing with their thoughts. If their attention wanders, they forcibly bring it back to the breath. Too much forcing is not the Middle Way. The Middle Way is the ease that arises naturally in the mind when there is right effort, right intention, and right awareness. When the practice is right and there is ease of mind, we can simply watch the different states that arise and consider their nature. We don't need to argue with anything. Arguing only causes restlessness. Whatever emotion arises is within the domain of our awareness, and we simply watch. Whether it's joyful or the absolute opposite, each experience is within the boundaries of our awareness. We just sit, watch, recognize, and contemplate them all. They will naturally cease. Why do they cease? Because that is their nature. It is this realization of the true nature of change that strengthens and stills the mind. With such insight there is tranquility and peace.

What we call "me" is merely a convention. We are born without names, then somebody gives us a name. After being called this name for a while, we start to think that a thing called "me and mine" actually exists. Then we feel we have to spend our whole lives looking after it. The wisdom of the Buddha knows how to let go of this "me," this "self," and all that pertains to it—possessions, attitudes, views, and opinions. This means letting go of the conditions that make suffering arise, and that requires taking the opportunity to see the true nature of things.

Recollecting Our Goodness

Ajahn Amaro • December 2008

When we're engaged in a lot of activity, we can become so focused on the details of what we're doing that we forget there's an element of generosity and goodness in our actions. When Ajahn Sumedho was a young monk, Luang Por Chah recommended that he recollect his good qualities. Ajahn Sumedho couldn't understand what Luang Por was talking about because his mind was quite busy and filled up with negative thoughts and emotional habits. He thought of himself as basically a selfish, nasty, horrible person, and an embarrassment to the robes.

Luang Por Chah told him, "If you're such a bad person and really evil, you wouldn't want to live with Buddhist monks. We would be the last people you would want to spend time with. If you're so off the mark and if your mind is so given to unwholesomeness, you wouldn't want to be around people who are honest, refrain from stealing, refrain from consuming intoxicants, people who don't behave in unruly ways. The last thing you'd want to do is be around virtuous people." When Luang Por said this to him, he was quite startled by it. He thought to himself, *You know that's true. I can easily forget that I'm living in a Buddhist monastery with Buddhist monks. There must be some reason why I'm doing this.*

We can become quite focused on our faults, wrongdoings, and the things we said that were less than generous, friendly, helpful, or patient. Even after someone has asked us for advice, what we think about later is how much better it would have been to have said this or that. *Oh, I really didn't get that right.* The attention goes to all our shortcomings, failures, and weaknesses, and we obsess on those qualities.

That's how it was for Ajahn Sumedho. So when Luang Por Chah suggested, "Why don't you recollect all of your good qualities?" there was no pigeonhole for him to put them in. At that time any good quality he had, he saw as inflated, egotistical, proud, or conceited. But Luang Por said, "No. This is *cāgānussati*, recollecting your goodness, recollecting your own generosity. It's a completely normal concept." Now, since we've had the good fortune to hear Laung Por Chah's advice to Ajahn Sumedho, it would behoove us to put that advice into practice for ourselves.

One way for us to do that is to recollect all the good effort we're making in looking after the kitchen, providing food, looking after the construction projects, the *kuṭis*, the buildings, or the micro-hydro project we're setting up. These are acts of generosity and kindness, of putting forth effort and putting forth our time to help other people. Many people have helped with the construction of the kuṭi down by the Bhikkhu Commons. Of those people, how many are actually going to live in it? Probably a very small proportion. The effort that we make is not simply in the single task we do, but also in the wholesomeness and goodness it supports—the *kusala kamma* it supports. By providing this dwelling, this food, these Dhamma talks, we bring enormous blessings into our lives.

Take Tan Ṭhitapañño, for instance. He's wrestling with the intricacies of the Expression Engine software and the obstructive passwords that won't let him use the program. When doing

24

such hard work, it can be easy to forget about the fact that there are people all over the planet who delight in what this work accomplishes, *Oh look, a new Dhamma talk on the Abhayagiri website. How marvelous! This is fantastic!* This isn't simply about trying to cheer ourselves up or look on the bright side. This really is the bright side. Earlier in the year a fellow came to Abhayagiri from Liverpool, England. He was so happy to be here. He didn't even stay for a full day. He happened to be in the country on holiday and took a chance to visit us. He said, "We have this little meditation group in Liverpool, and we listen to Abhayagiri talks all the time. It's so great to be here." He was bubbling with happiness. We can forget that our lives are connected with little groups of people like that all over the planet. In our small efforts to keep the bodies fed, to keep the shelters workable, to provide Dhamma talks on the website, to offer publications, to pay the bills—every little piece is bringing goodness into the world. That's kusala kamma, wholesome action.

It's not indulgence, egotism, or pride to be reflecting on that goodness. The Buddha himself encourages cāgānussati, recollecting our generosity, because that brightens and brings joy to the mind. We can take some time to recollect all the efforts that we're making on the practical front as well as with the formal meditation practice. The word *anumodanā* means rejoicing in the goodness that has been done. The cynical mind says, *Yeah, well, that's one thing. But I've really got some serious problems. Basically I'm just a defiled mess. I really am!* We need to listen to that voice with compassion, but at the same time, we don't want to let it run our lives. So we listen and then gently park it to one side. We can reflect, *Even if I'm filled with utterly ghastly defilements, still there are things I've done that have helped people.*

That's an undeniable fact. There's some goodness or brightness that I've brought into the lives of others. My effort to be a little bit more patient has benefited other beings. How wonderful! By letting that brightness inform our lives, we can be encouraged and gladdened by it.

Where Did That Self Go?

Ajahn Karuṇadhammo • December 2013

This morning we chanted the recollection of the "Thirty-Two Parts of the Body," as well as the Anattalakkhaṇa Sutta, which mentions thoughts, perceptions, and feelings. They can both be used to reflect on aspects of not-self.

The "Thirty-Two Parts of the Body" is a reflection that can be utilized to reduce sensual desire when there is a strong attachment to the human body as an object of attraction. We can also bring this reflection up as a way of dividing up what we usually consider a unit, a whole, something to attach a sense of self to. Oftentimes we identify with this body as either "me" or "mine," as something I possess or something that is actually who I am. The "Thirty-Two Parts of the Body" contemplation helps us tease the body apart so that we can reflect on how this body is just a collection of parts, any one of which we would be hard-pressed to say is who I am or "me." We can ask ourselves, *What would happen if I lost an arm or a leg or had a body part that had to be taken out because of disease? If I take something away from this body then what is left is different. So is this body any less me than it was before? Or is it a different me? Or perhaps it is not me at all?* That is one way that we can reflect on the "Thirty-Two Parts of the Body."

Our friend Iris's cancer has moved to her brain. Although she is having treatment, her perceptual world seems to have been altered in some ways. She perceives the world around her differently than she normally did or how we normally do. When we look at things in a different way or see different aspects or angles of physical and mental phenomena, it can help us see how much stock we put into the continuity of the perceptual realm. As the Anattalakkhaṇa Sutta suggests, we can see how we attach to our perceptions a sense of "me," "myself," and "who I am." This continuity of thoughts, perceptions, and feelings weaves a web of self and sometimes gets changed or altered or diminished. *Where did that "me" go to? Where did that self go? Is it a different one? Is it the same one but looked at from a different angle? Or is it possibly just another perception that I have weaved together to give a sense of security and stability?*

It is good to reflect on the change and instability of what we normally call "me" or "mine," both in the body and in the mind. We can take this up as a contemplation and examination, and ask ourselves, *Am I really any of these?*

Not Reaching for the Stars

Luang Por Pasanno • July 2013

In an ideal world, a summer day like this would be 80 degrees with a gentle breeze. In reality, it's 108 degrees, and the air is not moving at all. How do we handle the contrast between what is ideal and what is real? We can moan and whinge or retreat into fantasy and desire, but from the Buddha's perspective, it's always about establishing a sense of clarity and equanimity within the reality of the present moment.

With something like the weather, it's fairly easy for us to see our unrealistic hopes clearly and accept them for what they are. But in other areas, it's more difficult. For instance, living as we do in a spiritual community, we may hold to a utopian notion that everyone here should be mindful, peaceful, contented, and harmonious. And it's true—we should be. But we can keep in mind that this "should" is based on an ideal. The reality is oftentimes quite different. So it's necessary to learn how to navigate those times when we, or others, aren't living up to the elevated principles that we hold. To do that, we can reflect on whether it's realistic to expect everybody to live up to our lofty notions simply because these notions are what we would like or prefer. We can reflect on how well we personally adapt and respond to the realities of our existence and see that it is often difficult to live up to our *own* ideas of perfection.

This doesn't mean we should throw out all the ideals we have and tell ourselves to forget it. Holding to wholesome ideals can be a skillful thing to do. But we need to be very cautious of measuring ourselves against those high values all the time. Doing that exacerbates dissatisfaction, discontent, and a sense of suffering.

In former times, navigation at sea depended on frequently checking the stars with a sextant to set and maintain a realistic course of direction. It wasn't about trying to reach the stars! In a similar way, as practitioners we merely need to set ourselves on a wholesome, skillful course; we don't need to constantly frustrate ourselves or others by trying to comply with unrealistic notions of perfection. Usually our ideals—even wholesome ones—are filled with wishful thinking and fantasy. So it's important to ground our elevated standards in reality. By doing that, we can find a realistic course of action that supports our living skillfully. Applying the Dhamma in our day-to-day lives, we can learn to live with each other and with ourselves in a beneficial, wholesome way.

Determined to Suffer

Ajahn Yatiko • July 2012

We suffer because we are not seeing things with the right perspective.

We're here in this monastery by choice, and all the work is done on a voluntary basis. It's a good place. Within this sort of environment, there is no need to suffer. Things are the way they are. But through it all, we still seem to have an insatiable need to suffer. We are absolutely determined to not let go or soften our perspective. It's as if we'd rather suffer than grow. The problem is we don't realize that suffering is going to grow and grow and grow. Eventually we are going to have to let go of all the situations that cause suffering, such as loss, physical pain, uncertainty, or whatever it is we don't like. It's just the way it is.

The fact that we experience a particular object as something we don't like is because of the way we structure our values and priorities *within*. None of what we experience from the outside—be it community, people, activities, or responsibilities—has an objective, factual existence. It's something that we experience through our internal senses. We give meaning to things and, based on the meaning we give, we attach to this and hate that. We create an entire world out of what we experience, and we end up *living* in that world. The world, as we know it, isn't actually out there; it's in our heads. Understanding this helps us to see that our suffering is coming from our own actions, views, and decisions and not from the outside.

This sort of reflection is empowering because it puts us in control. There's really nothing and no one else we can blame. This truth is especially apparent when we live in a monastery like this. It's good enough to carry out our practice. Perhaps it's not so apparent for people immersed in a cultural setting—local or global—where ethics are not a priority and introspection is not encouraged or valued. In that situation, it's easier to convince ourselves that our choices and actions are taking place in an external world.

But that perspective doesn't hold sway in the environment we have here. So we can surrender to the situation, the routine, the principles, and the practices of the monastery and learn to let go. Through that quality of surrender, the heart starts to feel a sense of release. We start to gain a sense of confidence as to what the spiritual life is really about and what's important in our life.

Containing the Chicken

Luang Por Pasanno • August 2012

The theme we used for Upāsikā Day yesterday was brightening the mind and focusing on the ten *anussati*—the ten recollections: Buddha, Dhamma, Saṅgha, virtue, generosity, celestial beings, mindfulness of the body, mindfulness of death, mindfulness of breathing, and Nibbāna—peace. Several people expressed their appreciation for being taught about the ten recollections in that it gave them more freedom and flexibility to work with the mind.

Meditation can often become mechanical or method oriented, or focus solely on concentration and trying to get the mind to stop thinking. Sometimes when we practice like this, there tends to be a lot of effort expended, and this can agitate the mind. However, the Buddha taught ways of using the thought process so that it supports the cultivation of wholesome and bright states of mind. Thinking in this way naturally leads the mind to settle down. The mind naturally settles when it feels good, when there's a quality of well-being. We encourage this by bringing to mind directed thought and attention and evaluating the result of that. When we do this, there can be a continuity of wholesome and skillful thoughts, and the mind can become settled and clear.

Ajahn Chah said that meditation is like containing a chicken. In a village, when a person has a chicken and is concerned that it's going to run off, he gets a loosely-woven large bamboo basket and plunks it over the chicken. Rice can be put in the basket, and the chicken stays in the container. One doesn't have to tie the chicken down or keep it from taking a step anywhere. Having a container for the chicken is sufficient. In the same way, when the mind is imbued with a sphere of awareness and intention, and attention is being directed on a wholesome theme, then the mind will stay within that container. It doesn't mean that it's forced to stay there, but it's content within that sphere. These recollections are a skillful means of directing attention, bringing wholesome recollections to the mind so it will settle within that container.

Both in our formal meditation practice and throughout the day we can bring to mind and recollect the Buddha, the Dhamma, the Saṅgha, virtue, generosity, celestial beings, the body, death, the breath, and Nibbāna—peace. Another helpful theme that is not on this list is the quality of saṃvega, spiritual urgency or a chastening of worldly tendencies. This can help remind us of death and the limitations of the body. A complementary theme for saṃvega is to set up the intention to put forth effort, to realize what the Buddha taught and the example that he set. Another important quality that comes to mind is pasāda, which is a sense of serene confidence and clarity of well-being; it has a joyful sense to it.

We want to encourage these ten recollections in our practice as well as these other skillful qualities so that we create a wholesome foundation for the mind. We have a lot of space to experiment and work with these themes. As we get to know them, we can see what works and what helps the mind direct itself toward the Dhamma.

Skills for Letting Go

Ajahn Ñāṇiko • December 2013

In our practice we are normally working with the core defilements of greed, anger, and delusion. Often when these defilements arise, the way we deal with them is through restraint. When we restrain the defilements it feels different than actually letting them go. With restraint, we continue to experience the defilement; it's an undercurrent in the mind. By contrast, when we genuinely let something go, there is a feeling of being completely refreshed and replenished. There can be an experience in both the body and the mind of being filled with a clear, cool, pure substance. Restraint is important as well, however. When there is irritation or anger in the mind, or a nagging desire that won't go away, we can first use restraint as an antidote by applying, for example, *mettā* or *asubha* practices. The mind will then loosen its grip on these defilements and let go.

Sometimes we may think it's impossible for the mind to let go, but it is important that we not think this way. The mind will let go in its own time according to its conditioning and its kamma. In particular, letting go depends on the kamma of our skillful effort in the practice. We don't need to figure out when the mind will let go, we just keep practicing. Walking, standing, sitting, or lying down, we keep the Dhamma teachings in mind, moving forward with faith that true letting go is possible. It is not helpful to tell ourselves, *I don't have enough pāramī to let go.*

Letting go is a skill. Everyone has to put forth effort, especially when we are just beginning.

Learning how to fail is another important part of the letting-go practice. About a month ago I was trying to fix an old planer. It was difficult to get the blade removed. I was in the shop with Doug, and I told him, "I'm prepared to fail at this, but I'll give it a try." There was one screw with a stripped head, and after awhile I finally managed to remove it. I was so excited when I took it out that I forgot to take out the other screw that didn't have any problems. I started prying the blade out and ended up breaking the planer entirely. Afterward I reviewed my mind, and I thought, *I told Doug that I was prepared to fail at this, but actually I wasn't prepared to fail at all.* I spent the next three days mired in *dukkha,* full of reproach about my foolish mistake. It took quite a while to let that one go. So it's important to learn how to fail without taking it personally. After all, taking things personally is the very thing we're learning to let go of.

Faith Develops Energy and Wisdom

Luang Por Pasanno • June 2012

Faith is an essential part of our practice, and it's not something that magically appears on its own. Rather, the arising of faith takes effort. We need to direct our attention toward it, to frequently reflect on the arising of faith as a real possibility for us.

As Westerners, most of us are not on familiar ground when we reflect on faith. But it is an important quality for balancing the different aspects of our practice. In particular, faith comes first among the five spiritual faculties. It is used to balance wisdom, the fifth faculty, and to support energy and effort—the second faculty. How does that work? Wisdom arises from investigative analysis, and, without faith, investigative analysis becomes dry, and we tend to lose energy. The qualities of faith include confidence and devotion, both of which naturally result in increased energy and effort. Energy and effort need to be nourished, and faith is an important part of that nourishment.

The opposite is true as well: When the wisdom faculty is lacking in faith, it often leads to cleverness and a superficially critical way of evaluating things. Without faith, wisdom can increase our negativity, which in turn can reduce our own energy and the energy of the people we engage with.

For many reasons, it is important to turn our attention toward faith, to reflect on it, so we can recognize faith as an essential part of our practice.

Mindfulness of Death, Appreciation for Life

Ajahn Karuṇadhammo • May 2013

Luang Por Pasanno mentioned that Debbie's mother is going to be signing into the palliative and hospice care programs because her condition is deteriorating. I would think Debbie has been practicing with death contemplation as this is happening, particularly after she lost her sister-in-law a few months ago. The Buddha encouraged us to reflect daily and remind ourselves that death can come at any time. It's easy to externalize, *It's happening to somebody else, not me.* But at some point, it won't be somebody else, it will be us, and it would be nice to think that we are ready for it when it comes. This isn't meant to be a morbid reflection, but more an encouragement to contemplate death, bringing us closer to the reality of it and to encourage a sense of heedfulness and urgency in the practice.

It's so easy to get lost in the tasks of the day, particularly as we are about to launch into a work period. I would imagine that a significant number of people right now are thinking about the tasks they need to do. I find myself doing that sometimes as well. But we can pull back a bit and remind ourselves, *Hold on a second, life is precious. I don't know when or how I'm going to die. If death occurred for me right now, would I be ready for it? Would there be remorse? Are there things that I have done or left undone that I would regret if I died today?* We can take a few moments

39

to contemplate the potential immediacy of death and see what this might bring up for us. Contemplating death in this way allows us to clarify what is precious in our lives which frees us from the tendency to get lost in the details. This in turn helps us focus on what our priorities are. So instead of death contemplation producing a negative feeling such as fear or bewilderment, we can be moved to a sense of lightness and release as we focus on what is most important to us. A life well lived, focused on what is most meaningful for us, has the greater potential to be a life free of regret and remorse.

Death is a present-moment experience; it's not in the future. When the moment of death arrives, it will be just that moment—everything before that moment of death is still life, with all of its projections, worries, and fears, including the fear of that approaching death. But when death actually occurs, it is just one brief moment. So at the moment of death, death is now. Before that moment, it is just a projection. With contemplation of death we become more familiar with this inevitable ending so that when it finally comes, we are prepared for it, neither afraid of it or confused with this very ordinary present-moment experience.

If we keep that in mind then we do not really have any other option than to contemplate what's going on for us right here and right now. It's the only place we are going to be ready when it's time for the body to move on, for the elements to dissolve. For most of us, one of the best ways to do this is by using mindfulness of the body. We can notice the position of the body, the posture of the body—standing, walking, sitting, and lying down. This is the most basic contemplation of the body, and we can maintain it when we are doing just about anything—constantly coming back and asking ourselves, *What is the posture of the body? What is the disposition of the body? If it's moving, how is it moving through space?* We can know what's happening with the arms, the legs, the head, the torso, and be present with the body. We can also incorporate the mood of the mind, *What's the mood like right here and right now?* If we keep on attending to right here and right now as we go through our daily activities, then when it comes time for death to greet us, we will be ready right there and right then to be aware of the event as it happens. Bringing mindfulness right here and right now and reminding ourselves of the preciousness of this human life is a great way of reducing fear and anxiety and establishing a sense of purpose along the path.

Truthfulness in Speech

Ajahn Yatiko • June 2013

One way we are generous with each other here at the monastery is in the realm of truthful speech—an attribute that is essential in one who is walking the Buddha's path. The notion of truthful speech is deep and profound. It doesn't simply mean saying things that are truthful; it also implies expressing ourselves honestly—being able to clearly communicate with others, even when there's a thorny issue at hand.

Sometimes our attempts at communicating can be hopelessly indirect, which is not helpful. For example, if we feel somebody is being unkind to us, rather than letting them know, we might instead ostentatiously increase our "kindness" around them, hoping they'll get the message and change. This rarely works and can sometimes be seen as passive-aggressive. So it's important to establish genuinely truthful speech to directly express our needs to others, at the appropriate time, so they can hear and understand us. This takes practice, but it's very much a part of the path.

More generally, it is also important to act with a generous heart, no matter what we're doing. This requires an attitude of taking responsibility, recognizing that all institutions—families, monasteries, and communities of all kinds—require people to take responsibility, to open their eyes, and to see what needs to be done to help others.

Sometimes when we see somebody in need, physically or emotionally, we may think to ourselves, *Well, this is a big place, and someone else will take care of the situation.* When we think in this way, it's as if we are placing an invisible force field around those who are in need so we can't see them or their problems. Ajahn Amaro has colloquially referred to this phenomenon as if people are approaching the world with an "SEP field"—a somebody-else's-problem field. In a large community like this, it can be easy to take the SEP field approach and ignore the problems of visitors or those we live with. But we mustn't let these people slip through the cracks or fall by the wayside. This requires a resolve to help those in need as best we can and not just for their sake. Our holding to such a resolve will help improve the overall sense of well-being, functionality, coherence, harmony, and brightness in the community we're living in.

An Auspicious Day of Blessings

Luang Por Pasanno • July 2012

Today is Friday the 13th, and by tradition some people believe that it's an unlucky day. Many people have different ideas of why Friday the 13th became known as an unlucky day. In the Thai tradition and the Asian tradition in general, there are lucky days, unlucky days, auspicious and inauspicious times. Ajahn Chah used to say that whatever day we are doing something wholesome, that is an auspicious day. He also said there is no such thing as a day in and of itself that is inauspicious or unlucky. We are completely dependent on gathering our own resources into doing something that is skillful, beneficial, and wholesome. So the opportunity for doing that which is wholesome is in itself what makes it a blessing in the world. The Pāli word *mahāmaṅgala* means the highest blessings. The Mahāmaṅgala Sutta encourages the cultivation of that which is skillful: association with good people and developing inner virtues that are beneficial to both ourselves and others (Sn 2.4). When we cultivate these virtues, we create the blessings of a skillful life, sharing those blessings with the people we're living with and the people we come into contact with. That is how we bring great blessings into the world.

Non-Contention Is Full Awareness

Ajahn Amaro • December 2002

Under the Bodhi tree the Buddha's response to death—in the form of Māra's threats, cajolings, temptations, and attempts to cause doubts—was not life-affirmation, going into a deep state of concentration to evade Māra, blasting him with a *vajra* bolt, trying to be reasonable and negotiate on Māra's terms, or trying to justify himself. Instead, the Buddha's response was a fearless wakefulness. Almost invariably, throughout the accounts of the Buddha's meetings with Māra, as soon as he is aware of the malefactor's presence, he says: "I know you, Māra." And the game is over.

Maybe this is a myth or maybe not, but such tales maintain their power through their congruity with truth as we experience it. When Māra knows the Buddha has seen the hook inside the bait, he knows his victim is not going to bite. Māra is defeated in that gesture of knowing. This suggests that the opposite of death is not birth, life-affirmation, or the destruction of death. Rather, the opposite of death is wakefulness.

Perhaps the most meaningful way of considering the encounters between the Buddha and Māra is to regard them as depicting the arising of unwholesome, ego-based states in the mind of the Buddha. They portray the instinctual fears, doubts, and desires that arise, but have no place to land. When using the myth as a map of our own psyches, Māra represents our ego-death experiences—loneliness, anger, obsessiveness, greed, and doubt—and the Buddha's example points the way for our hearts to respond most skillfully with a wise, wakeful, and radical non-contention. As soon as we contend against death, we've bought into Māra's value system and bitten his hook—when we hate and fear death, or want to swamp it with life, Māra has won. We have "gone over to Māra's side, and the Evil One can do with [us] as he likes" (SN 35.115). We can perhaps run with his line for a while, but sooner or later Māra is going to reel us in.

Non-contention is not a passivity, a denial, or a switching off—numbly suffering the slings and arrows as they thump into us. Rather, non-contention is full awareness. The Buddha doesn't say "It's okay Māra, do your worst, I won't stand in your way." No, the point is to defeat Māra—but the way we defeat him is by not contending against him. In one of the most often quoted passages of the Dhammapada, the Buddha states, "Hatred does not cease by hatred, but by love alone. This is an eternal truth" (Dhp 5).

The Simplicity of Buddho

Luang Por Pasanno • June 2005

These last two weeks were supposed to be a time of retreat for me, but it didn't quite end up that way. I had to catch up on work and help out with some of the construction. While I was working, something came to mind that I found very fruitful: To work with the busyness—the activity that I was involved in—I returned to the very simple practice of repeating the word *Buddho*. Buddho is the name of the Buddha. It means "to awaken" or "to be awake." It's a basic, foundational practice that is used throughout Thailand, particularly in the northeast. I used that short mantra in conjunction with the breath. On the in-breath, "Bud," on the out-breath, "dho."

The mind is so easily attracted to proliferation and embellishment: *Give me a story, a drama, something to bite into—give me anything, so long as I can play the starring role.* When we recite Buddho, we are not feeding, encouraging or supporting the embellishment and dramatization of experience.

On the in-breath, "Bud," on the out-breath, "dho,"—it's simple and helpful. Because it is the name of the Buddha, it's a reminder of bringing the presence of the Buddha into each in-breath and each out-breath. It's bringing the recollection of the Buddha—both as the teacher and as the archetype of the enlightened being—into the heart, the mind, and consciousness.

Buddho is a powerful presence because it cuts through our tendency to fill the mind with worries, concerns, desires,

47

fantasies, proliferations, ideas, ideals, views, and opinions. All this clutter is the antithesis of the enlightened being. We can remember that by using this simple word. On the in-breath, "Bud." On the out-breath, "dho."

Letting Go of a Defilement

Ajahn Yatiko • July 2012

Ajahn Liem is known for working all day long and encouraging the monastic community to contribute a great deal of work and service. That's a big part of his teachings. But how well does it fit with our practice here? When we are away from our *kuṭis*, many of us carry with us the desire to return to our kuṭis right away and continue our formal practice of sitting and walking meditation. Suppose a senior monk tells us that the monastery just received a very large shipment of books, and that we'll need to help out with that as soon as the meal ends until eight o'clock at night. What would be our internal response?

As monastics, we're to set our intention toward staying aware of the present moment and letting go of our attachments to the future and past. That's what it means to be mindful and use wisdom in daily life. We open to the present moment and abandon any notion of the future. In a monastic environment like this, we're encouraged to let the future take care of itself. We let go and do whatever is needed, whatever comes up. Wherever there's an opportunity to serve or work, we do that. We simply let go of the future. In a monastic environment, we can do that because we trust that there will be plenty of time for formal practice when the time is right.

When we are able let go of the past and future, we are letting go of our fears, fixed views, attachments, and desires—we are letting go of our defilements. This is a profound experience.

We can study all we want about Buddhism and have incredible knowledge of the scriptures in Pāli. We can even write a book on mindfulness, but still not know what mindfulness is or how to let go of a basic defilement. These are some of the most important aspects of the path—to practice mindfulness and understand how to let go of defilements. That's much more valuable than knowing all the suttas.

So we use every moment throughout the day to practice letting go—when we get back to our kuṭis and are doing walking and sitting meditation, when we are eating, when we are working and doing service—whether things are going well or not. We do this with a sense that the future doesn't exist, by opening to the present moment and doing whatever comes to hand. If nothing comes to hand, then we do walking or sitting meditation, remaining in the present, moment by moment, letting go of everything else. That's how we can build a strong and stable foundation for the arising of insight and the development of the path.

The Intruding Sense of Self

Luang Por Pasanno • July 2013

It is uncanny how the sense of self tends to intrude on everything, whether it is in our meditation, when we are working,
doing chores, in a group or by ourselves. That sense of self
keeps rearing its ugly head and creates suffering and a burden that we carry with us. Sometimes we think that coming to
live and practice in a monastery is solely about relinquishing
the world, but the heart of relinquishment is giving up of the
self and the perception of self. Upon very close examination,
the feeling, the projection, and the perception of self is nothing more than smoke and mirrors and does not have any real
substance.

We have this self-referential obsession: comparing ourselves to others, worrying about how we are doing, how others perceive us or how we perceive ourselves in relationship to
the past, present, and future, and it becomes incredibly convo-
luted. If we take a good look we can appreciate how much of
a burden all of this is. I believe this sense of self-obsession has
never been as strong as it is now in modern culture. Before,
most people's sense of self had to do with relationships—one's
relationship to family, village, or tribe. But in modern society
everything ends up being about *me*.

In our practice, we are trying to recognize this perception
of self, seeing how we keep buying into it, giving weight to that
feeling or perception, and recognizing that each building block

of self is simply an impermanent phenomenon. It isn't a matter of trying to get rid of the self or annihilating it in any way, because it's not something that is solid or substantial anyway. That's why we reflect on the five *khandhas*—form, feeling, perception, mental formations, and consciousness—seeing them as impermanent, unsatisfactory, and not-self. When we see the five khandhas for what they are, we gain insight into their true nature and let go of our investment in them, which is not a rejection or annihilation, but a clear seeing.

To be free of the world and worldly tendencies, we need to take leave of the world. Taking leave of the world means taking leave of the self-making, I-making habit. In the Buddha's idiom, when we buy into the notion of self, it is an affirmative action we are doing: *ahaṅkāra-mamaṅkāra-mānānusayā*, the I-making, my-making, based on the underlying tendency of conceit. It is the action of getting ourselves wrapped up in the perceptions of self and believing in these perceptions.

As we go about our day, we can reflect upon, investigate, and challenge these assumptions about the self and be willing to work with them over time. These assumptions are deeply ingrained in the mind, so examining them, making this process conscious, and being aware of that self-perspective is a central part of our practice.

Turning Inward With Patience

Ajahn Jotipālo • July 2013

I have been listening to a few of Bhikkhu Bodhi's talks on *mettā*, loving-kindness. He explained that in many practice situations, mettā can often be used with an external, outgoing energy and making a genuine wish for other people to be happy. However, there is also an internal response that can occur for us when we express mettā in this way.

I was surprised when Bhikkhu Bodhi mentioned that the word *khanti*, patience, is very closely related to the word *mettā*. I hadn't recognized that before. I have given a few talks on mettā and when I do, I often receive questions from people concerned with external circumstances, such as, "It's so painful to be with this person ..." or "When I'm in this situation it's really difficult. How do you deal with that?" Most of the questions are directed toward the practice of loving-kindness as a method for sending mettā outward. But we can also turn inward rather than outward. This is where Bhikkhu Bodhi says patience comes in. We can learn to turn toward the pain we feel—toward the dukkha we are experiencing in these difficult circumstances—and to hold that dukkha with a quality of patience.

Ajahn Sucitto once said that we often think of patience as waiting for change. *I will endure this situation, gritting my teeth, until it changes.* Certainly we might want a painful situation to change, but with true patience, according to Ajahn Sucitto, it's more like thinking, *I will be with this situation, period.* In other words, there's no expectation that the situation will change or get better.

By learning to turn toward our suffering and simply be with it, we are staying at the level of feeling. We are not getting into the story, the proliferation, or creating a self around it. If someone says something to us and we become angry or feel uncomfortable, instead of going outward, as we typically do with mettā, we can go inward. So when we feel pain in a situation, we can first recognize it. Then we move toward the painful feeling and explore it. If we can refrain from getting into the story behind the feeling, it will be that much easier to experience the feeling without wanting to change it. It's merely a physical sensation or a mental perception, and we do not need to add anything to it or try to make it go away. When we stay with a painful feeling in this way, we are experiencing khanti, true patience.

Problems From Nothing

Ajahn Yatiko • December 2012

If we were to look calmly and clearly at our experience living here in the monastery, we would see that our lives are extraordinarily simple. However, as human beings, we have this great penchant for creating problems out of nothing, a tendency that is quite self-harming. We create these problems with our perceptions and our desires. We pay attention to them, dwell on them, think about them, and obsess over them. So they stick with us. By dwelling on a particular issue, it grows and becomes more entrenched in our being and more entrenched in our perceptions. Before we know it, we're in a world that seems tremendously complicated, and we don't recognize that this is something we've created out of nothing. Behind these problems are nothing but our conflicted and contradictory desires.

With the path laid out for us by the Buddha, we can aim to see this process and explore how it is that we create these problems for ourselves. This is what will alleviate suffering and stress and ultimately prevent us from creating these complications in the first place. There's nothing here in the monastery that is a real concern. We have food to eat, water to drink— all our basic necessities are well taken care of. There's nothing that has to be done. Furthermore, we live in a harmonious community. Yet somehow we create a situation that seems so complicated. We all create these issues, from the most junior to the most senior of us. We can reflect on this and stop attending to things that we think are our personal dilemmas. We can observe this complicating and unnecessary process, put it down, and realize, *This is ridiculous, I don't have to suffer about this at all.* When we gain insight in this way, we come back to this peaceful, simple, spacious lifestyle that we're offered as renunciants.

The Impact of Right Speech

Ajahn Karuṇadhammo • April 2012

There are three ways we act on the inclinations, impulses, and intentions that come through the mind, and these are through body, speech, or mind. In a monastery, where there are many restraints on our activities, we can particularly notice the action of speech. Because actions and ideas are often expressed through speech, it's good to focus attention on this habit so we can learn about ourselves through our speech patterns. In the monastery we attempt to speak only the truth, but also to speak without anger, without tale-bearing, and without frivolous or unnecessary speech. Overall, people do a good job with the practice of right speech. However, speech is a difficult area of practice, and wrong speech can come out unexpectedly.

We come to the monastery with speech habits formed through family upbringing and the company we've kept. In Western cultures there can be an encouragement for people to express their thoughts openly, without considering how it might affect other people. This conditioning can manifest in speech indicative of trying to get one's way or get what one wants or being overly persistent. We can also express frustration, impress people, or present ourselves in certain ways that might be different from how we really are.

These habits in our minds can easily influence the speech we use in the monastery, and it can take constant vigilance to restrain ourselves from speaking in unskillful ways. Sometimes it's appropriate to say nothing, as when practicing noble silence. But at other times in a monastery there is a need for communication. We need to talk with each other to engender a sense of communal living and support as well as maintain harmony and well-being. If something needs to be communicated or somebody needs support, then skillful speech is appropriately encouraged. Nevertheless, we must watch the underlying impulse or mood in the mind that serves as the basis for speech. It's important to be careful with our speech because people are sensitive, and regrets can arise when others are hurt through the use of wrong speech. The Mettā Sutta suggests that we be not only straightforward in speech, but gentle as well. Even if our speech is true, we must be mindful of the impact our words have in a community, as well as when we are engaging in the world outside of the monastery.

The Generosity of Respect

Luang Por Pasanno • June 2005

When we are working together and interacting with each other, it's important for each of us in the community to have mutual respect for one another and to recognize that everybody is here because they have the intention to do something good, something wholesome. On the level of personality, it's easy to exercise our critical faculties—we're pretty adept at that. Especially when we live together over long periods of time, we get to know each others' quirks rather intimately. It doesn't take much intelligence or wisdom to pick up on somebody's quirks. It takes significantly more wisdom to attend to our own wholesome intentions and to honor and respect the wholesome intentions of other people. This doesn't mean that suddenly people are no longer irritating. But it does mean that we have a lot more space to deal with and support each other because we sense the opportunity for generosity—being generous by offering each other a sense of respect. We usually think of generosity in material terms, but it also means giving each other respect, space, encouragement, and support for our spiritual endeavors. That is a significant act of generosity that helps to transform the heart.

Stopping the Papañca Mill

Ajahn Amaro • August 2008

Papañca, a favorite theme of Ajahn Pasanno's, is that stream of incessant thinking, the flood of conceptual proliferation that the mind can so easily bring up. This produces an endless chatter of commentating, fretting, recollecting, recreating, planning, and imagining. The Buddha pointed to three particular qualities which are the driving forces behind these processes: craving, conceit, and views—the *papañca dhammas*. In the Anattalakkhaṇa Sutta—the Discourse on the Characteristic of Not-Self—he outlined these qualities in very simple terms. *Taṇhā*, craving, is defined as *etaṃ mama: This is mine. This belongs to me. This is my ladder, my chopping board, my space.* Next there's *eso'hamasmi:* the conceit "I am." *This is what I am. I am a person, I am tall, I am short, I am a woman, I am a man, I am old, I am young, I am a monk, I am a layperson. I am.* And lastly, there are views, *eso me attā: This is myself. This is me. This is my true nature.*

These are straightforward ways to define the forces that cause so much chaos in our lives and so many difficulties in our minds. The mind takes a simple perception with a given activity—walking along a path, picking up a length of pipe, chopping up some carrots, putting one's things away in a room, or any of the hundred little tasks of the day, and then runs with it: *This is what I'm doing. This is mine. Those are not his. Who's moved my shoes?* Or it identifies with ideas about who we are, for instance that we're weaker than others: *I'm pretty feeble, not nearly as strong as I used to be.* The mind takes simple feelings and perceptions—these habits of possessiveness and identification and uses them to fuel the objects of our six sense bases—what we see, hear, smell, taste, touch, and think. Then—whoosh!—off it all goes. The papañca erupts.

I often think of it like a mill. The papañca dhammas, possessiveness and identification, are like the engine that keeps the mill churning. We simply feed into the mill the objects of the six sense bases. And out of it pours papañca, the endless flow of mental chatter. We need to pay attention to the engine, to turn it off or stop giving it fuel, rather than getting lost in the stream of mental chatter—the commenting, regretting, planning, and inflating that goes on. Then the whole thing gets a lot quieter and more peaceful. The mind can clearly be aware of the present without creating this whole welter of confusion around it.

That's why it's very helpful that the Buddha pointed out these simple flags we can use to recognize when we're fueling the mill of papañca. If the mind is saying, *This is mine, this belongs to me, and that's yours;* if it's saying, *This is what I am, this is absolutely me and truly who and what I am,* then that's the signal to let go, to not get caught in that process, and to bring more spaciousness to the mind. As soon as the mind says, *That's mine, that's yours, I wish I had one of those, I'm like this, he's like that,* then that's the time to get suspicious. See the draw, the pull of that. We use the quality of mindfulness to notice the me-mine-yours flags and choose not to buy into them, not to fuel the engine.

When we're mindfully carrying out our tasks for the day, engaging with each other, functioning together as a community, dealing skillfully with what we see, hear, smell, taste, touch, and think, then the papañca mill engine doesn't have any fuel. It has nothing to power it. It simply sits there and causes no trouble. If we make the simple resolution to be mindful and apply effort to see how these papañca dhammas operate, and if we train ourselves not to buy into the I-making, my-making process, then we can save ourselves a great deal of difficulty. Life becomes far more harmonious and less complicated, and we can experience how pleasant and peaceful the mind can be.

The Present Moment and the Illusion of Time

Ajahn Yatiko • September 2012

When undertaking the life of a monastic, we have a direction and a goal in mind. There's something we're aiming for, and it's important to reflect on that with some frequency. From time to time we can ask ourselves, *What's the direction of my life? What's the goal of my life?*

We can also reflect on where this goal is located. With understanding we can see that it is located in the present moment. It's right now. Many of us live our lives thinking about the future most of the time. As we get older, we may think more and more about the past. But either way, we're not in the present moment. This is particularly apparent in our meditation, where the work is to bring our minds into the present and cut through the delusions we create around notions of time. The entire universe we attach to—what we like, dislike, dread, hate, fear, love—is a creation of our minds. We've created it in the present moment. Then we create this illusion of time and a whole universe of *saṃsāra*, which we feel trapped in. But the whole creation of time is something we do now, in the present moment.

Bringing the mind to the present moment is hard work, because, over the years, we have pursued the habit of creating time so that now this habit has great momentum and it keeps pushing us into the past and future. As a result, we could say, it takes a real balancing act to overcome that momentum—to bring ourselves back to a place that is centered and balanced in the present moment. Doing this is a matter of balance rather than effort.

When we see clearly, we know that there's only the present moment. That's all there has ever been. It takes commitment and determination to see this and take it seriously. There is no worldly benefit to be gained from returning to the present. No one else knows if we are in the present moment or not. No one will praise us for it, and we won't get any money for it—we don't get anything worldly out of it at all. But by continuing to return the mind to the present moment, we can eliminate having to bear the weight of the whole saṃsāric universe on our shoulders. No wonder coming back to the present is such a relief.

Appreciating the Goodness of Others

Luang Por Pasanno • June 2013

There are lots of us here living together in community, sharing the same space. So it's vital that we share the space harmoniously to ensure that things get done, like the external work of taking care of the monastery and the internal work of spiritual practice. To lay a foundation for living together harmoniously, there is a need to develop a sense of *kataññū*, which is usually translated as gratitude. Now the word *gratitude* is a bit loaded in the West, sort of like somebody is standing behind us waving his finger saying, "You should be grateful." That's quite a repelling image, and it doesn't convey the real essence of kataññū, which is the faculty within us that recognizes and appreciates the goodness of others.

It's important to exercise this faculty of kataññū to counteract the mind's tendency to focus on the things that irritate us, the flaws, the unskillful tendencies. That's where our minds go, and we tend to weigh ourselves down with negativity. I'm not suggesting we ignore or gloss over the shortcomings we see. Rather, this is about moving away from pointless negativity and, instead, recognizing and paying attention to the things people do that are skillful and wholesome.

Living in a monastery as we do, it's easy to take for granted the fundamental goodness of others. Goodness can seem so ordinary to us—it's part of the culture we live in here, and the standards we keep in that regard are quite high. We may need to make a deliberate effort to keep recognizing this "ordinary" goodness and to engender a sense of gratitude for its presence. We make the effort to do this because this gratitude nourishes our ability to live skillfully, and it helps establish wholesome states of mind. With our meditation, it's much easier to become peaceful when this quality of gratitude is present in the mind as opposed to when we experience negativity, which turns the mind toward all the flaws we perceive in everyone. So pay attention to gratitude—kataññū. Learn to appreciate the goodness of others, which will have the most beneficial results for our practice and well-being.

Physical Therapy for the Mind

Ajahn Karuṇadhammo • July 2013

Recently I've made visits to a physical therapist because I have
some ongoing muscle issues that have plagued me for the last
twenty years. Often this type of situation originates with a
small abnormality that causes pain, and many people will sub-
consciously allow the body to adjust to it or slump in a certain
way to relieve that pain. Although this gives temporary relief, it
turns out that people have adjusted their posture in a way that
ends up perpetuating the problem. Then they adjust a small
amount more to relieve more pain when it returns and, not too
long after, they find themselves misaligned. All of the small ad-
justments they've made while seeking temporary relief simply
do not take care of the condition. They're left with a posture
that is unbalanced, and it places additional stress on the bones,
muscles, and connective tissues that are responsible for good
alignment. The only way to correct the condition is to incorporate appropriate physical therapy and exercise to address all
of the changes that have taken place over the years. The body
is so accustomed to coping with the condition in a particular
manner that they have to unlearn those coping strategies and
go through some conscious discomfort to begin achieving the
goal of long-term healing.

I thought about this in line with how the mind works, the
way we usually buy into our moods, both the positive and the
negative ones. We find ourselves swinging back and forth in a

67

yo-yo-like manner, being drawn to and believing in the salvation of our positive moods and then, when they fade, reacting quite aversively to the negative ones. We can end up getting lost in the entire process. Each time we respond by moving toward an enjoyable mood or away from a disagreeable one, we're seeking a temporary solution to a long-term problem. The solution is having a sense of equanimity so that we are not constantly buying into and reacting to these different moods that pass through the mind.

This is similar to the way habits develop in the body. In the mind, an event happens. It triggers a perception—a habitual way of looking at an experience. That reminds us of something similar in the past, and we react in the same way through either aversion or attraction. Something can be unpleasant—a difficult situation that causes discomfort, unpleasantness, or aversion, and if we react to it automatically based on a past perception, it then reinforces the tendency to buy into old ways of reacting negatively. On the other hand, if it's something we are desirous of or excited about, that reinforces the tendency to go for it. Over time, we develop specific temporary coping strategies and react automatically in certain ways. We say, do, or think something, or we may internalize the experience with anger, blame, self-criticism, greed, fear, or confusion. Every time these coping strategies arise, they reinforce the original pattern that began the process in the first place. They seem to give some temporary relief for a period of time, but in the long run, they simply don't do the trick to relieve us of long-term suffering and pain.

Before those automatic responses come into play, we can spend time at the level of perception and feeling, using

68

mindfulness and clear comprehension to observe the response as it is occurring. We do this by allowing ourselves to experience the discomfort of an unskillful habit as we get to know and examine our reactions. This helps us refrain from automatically repeating the same old pattern. It also gives us time to respond with more wisdom and skillfulness based on having seen and understood the reaction clearly. As with physical therapy for the body, we can unlearn habits that have caused long-term unwholesome reactions in the mind. We just need to be willing to pause and observe the space around our uncomfortable experiences.

An Opportunity to
Develop Mindfulness

Luang Por Pasanno • July 2012

The Buddha spoke about the different postures for meditation—walking, sitting, standing, and lying down— basically every position of the body. He also spoke about the "foundations of mindfulness," that is, the body, feelings, the mind, and objects of mind. These are all supports we can use to develop attention. We have the opportunity to cultivate mindfulness and attention with everything we do. Specifically, we can use work and engagement in activity as a way to help with that cultivation.

As we develop mindfulness around our work chores, we can see that the functions and benefits of mindfulness are more than merely internal. For example, mindfulness enhances our ability to act more appropriately when in proximity with others who are also working. If we are painting next to somebody standing on a ladder, how do we maintain mindfulness so we don't knock them over? How do we engage in a conversation while wielding a paintbrush without splattering the person next to us? This sounds basic, but I've seen "mindful meditators" get into all sorts of trouble.

We can cultivate attention and mindfulness by anchoring our work meditation in the body. One way to do this is to ask ourselves, *How am I feeling? Am I relaxed and grounded? Am I in contact with things around me? Am I in contact with attention and awareness?*

In terms of other people nearby, we want to stay mindful of the need we all have for personal space. It takes a certain degree of empathy to understand that other people have their own comfort zones and to mindfully account for that. And while not wanting to be encroached upon, most people also have a wish to be recognized. This gives us a purpose and an opportunity to extend kind attention when relating to each other through our actions and speech. During the work periods, we can offer each other support and respect as human beings. That's how we engender loving-kindness and one of the many ways we cultivate mindfulness.

It is important to recognize the practical applications of mindfulness and how mindfulness affects our attitudes and perspectives, both in how we relate to others and to the world around us. From something very simple like being mindful of one breath at a time, one step at a time, we can start to develop a foundation in clarity and learning, which brings much benefit into our lives.

Putting Forth Effort

Ajahn Yatiko • June 2012

For both monastics and laypeople visiting the monastery, it is helpful to reflect on sustenance, what it is that sustains us materially. Laypeople offer food to the monastery, and we eat this food. They work some eight hours a day, five days a week or more, at a job that can often be unpleasant. It's hard work, and they call it work because it *is* work. For most people the mind inclines toward not doing this work. People would rather be relaxing, sitting out under the sun and taking it easy, but they can't do that. They have to work, because they have to support themselves and sustain their lives. Many people come to this monastery on a regular basis with food they've bought using the fruits of their own labor. We eat and depend on this offered food every day at the monastery, so we have a very direct relationship with the work laypeople do.

As a result, we have a responsibility to practice; our practice is why we are being offered food. Laypeople want to support the monastery so that we will grow in the Dhamma and lessen our greed, hatred, and delusion. Ajahn Dtun once said that we should be meditating at least eight hours a day, because that's the amount of time laypeople put into their workday, and for many of them it's even more than that. I think that at Abhayagiri eight hours a day of formal practice would be difficult, because we have a lot happening, especially in the mornings with our work period and chores. However, we can still think

72

of this eight hours in the sense of making sure that mindfulness is present for that amount of time—actually, for the entire day. During this time we're not simply following our moods and opinions, we are going against the grain and putting forth effort to decrease the defilements.

Some of us may feel dispirited when we hear about putting forth effort, because it sounds heavy to us, and we may not want to put forth a lot of exertion. However, whether we like it or not, it is something we have to do; it is simply part of the deal, part of what monastic life is all about. If putting forth effort is something we don't want to do, then monastic life might not be for us. It is a life of effort, and it requires resolution and struggle. We should keep that in mind.

But the situation is not bleak. In the beginning stage of making an effort, there is a hump we have to get over, but then it gets easier. There are three phases of effort. In the first phase, energy needs to be aroused, and this requires discipline and exertion. In the second phase, once energy is aroused and established, the effort maintains itself, to a certain extent, because of that established energy. The third phase is known as being unshakable, where nothing can stop the effort and energy until the goal is achieved. The first phase is the most difficult, because it takes a lot of strength and resolution simply to get things going. It's like a rocket that's leaving the atmosphere; it takes an enormous amount of fuel to overcome the pull of Earth's gravity, but once it gets into space then it can coast for awhile. It's a bit the same with the energy and effort we put into our practice.

Through this entire process, especially the first phase, it is extremely helpful to hold the attitude and perception

∨ that making an effort is actually *pleasant*. If effort is exercised properly, the experience of effort is enjoyable, invigorating—something we can learn to delight in. If we don't take delight in putting forth effort, then it is quite an unpleasant experience. So we need to learn how to experience the pleasant side of effort. We can start with a simple and direct reflection: *In what way can I put forth and sustain effort so that it is enjoyable, fulfilling, and nurturing to both my practice and to my heart?*

Being Comfortable Is Not the End of Suffering

Luang Por Pasanno • August 2013

There's an element of the human psyche that is constantly looking for comfort, security, and ease. We can sometimes believe that the end of suffering is when we bring about the circumstances in which we don't have to extend ourselves or put forth too much effort. But even when we've managed to manipulate conditions in a way that allows us to feel relatively comfortable and laid back, we inevitably realize that we are still suffering.

That's why, as practitioners, we need to be willing to stretch our capabilities and constantly look for ways that help us to do that. Whether we're on retreat or engaged with each other in the monastery's communal routine, we need to keep experimenting and working with different practices to stretch ourselves further.

Of course, there should be a balance in our efforts; constantly pushing and striving is itself a form of suffering. This is why the Buddha pointed to the Middle Way. Rather than investigating what it is that makes us feel relatively comfortable and secure, we can investigate what it is that undermines the tendencies of greed, hatred, and delusion. We need to look very carefully, asking ourselves, *What are those underlying roots of delusion? What are those habits of selfishness?*

By investigating like this, we learn that we don't need to be tripped up by our habits or defilements; we learn to let go of our comfort-seeking and to undermine the underlying tendencies ✓ that cause us complication and difficulty; and we learn to be okay with whatever conditions arise. When we have stretched our capabilities this far, we can find true ease and comfort that is independent of any causes or conditions.

Abhayagiri Is Complete

Ajahn Amaro • November 2012

I'm experiencing a very worldly delight in non-involvement, non-responsibility. It's lovely to be here as a visitor, not having to feel responsible for making all the threads come together, as I did before leaving for Amaravati a couple years ago. But it's also important to note—especially during the busy festival season we're in right now—that the complications that are difficult are not the external ones, like the logistical nightmares the work monk has to deal with. It's the logistical nightmares *inside* that are the real troublemakers. It's always good to bring that to mind. It's not the external complications that really make things difficult, it's the way we pick things up, create complications, and tangle things within ourselves. That's the real cause of tension, of *dukkha*, of stress within.

Every monastery is the same during the festival season. It draws together a large, complex array of different tasks that need to be taken care of with so many extra people lending a hand while also being part of the mix. As Luang Por Pasanno was saying yesterday, we need to lean into the wind in a very conscious way so as to counteract the tendency we have to create inner complication, because there's such a great potential during this time for getting caught up, being busy, resentful, or excited.

Yesterday, when some of us were walking around with Tan Ṭhitābho in the morning, we saw many new *kuṭis* and the new workshop which were all built over the last couple of years since I departed. These were things that Luang Por Pasanno, myself, and others would fantasize about. *It'd be a nice place to have a kuṭi there, or we could do this here, or maybe we should put the workshop there.* Many of these things have suddenly become a reality. Of course, these physical changes took place slowly and steadily over time. So much has evolved since June 1st, 1996 when I, along with Anagārika Tom, now Ajahn Karuṇadhammo, Debbie, and a gang of others rolled up to the newly purchased property. On that very first evening, once we'd cleaned up the house, set up the domed tents that we'd be living in, gotten ourselves sorted and settled, I remember thinking, *Now the monastery is complete, now it is done.*

With those words, I was taking a leaf out of Luang Por Liem's book. I remember when preparations were underway for Luang Por Chah's funeral. For his cremation, a very large Buddhist memorial structure, called a *cetiya*, was under construction. A whole new eating hall, road system, water towers, and more than 630 toilets were all under construction simultaneously. During that time, there was someone who was touring the monastery and saw all these different construction projects. He was quite amazed and bewildered. He then saw Luang Por Liem, who was running the whole show and had just come down off of the roof of a large building with a welding torch in hand. The man said to Luang Por, "This is incredible, this is amazing, there's so much happening here. I bet you'll be really glad when it's finished." And Luang Por Liem responded in his inimitable Luang Por Liem way, "I finish it every day." That is a very simple observation, but coming from Luang Por Liem, it's not merely a nice thing to say. It's not just sophistry;

it's the actuality. Yes, we have bare girders here and wet concrete over there and so many pits for the concrete rings to go in under all of these toilets, and they are all sitting out there in heaps. But it's completely finished, just as it is. This is what it is, right now.

When there's a lot of activity going on—going from here to there, finding this and taking it over there, picking up these gas bottles and moving them over there, taking them to the wrong place and then taking them back—there can be a current or flood of becoming, what is called the *ogha* of becoming, which can be very intense. So it is important during the flow of activity to be leaning into the wind, to be leaning against that.

When we do something as simple as fill up the gas tank, we can think, *Okay, now Abhayagiri is complete. Everything is fully completed. Everything is done.* We reflect in that way, even though part of our worldly instinct might say, *Yeah but, but, but, look at my list! I have so many things to do, and they are important, and they have my name on them, and I can't just brush them away.* But with the reflection, *Abhayagiri is complete,* we can keep that worldly perspective in its appropriate place and recognize that, within a larger context, it's just as Luang Por Liem was expressing: it's finished. Even when the gas tank is half filled, it's finished. As you're carrying along the carpets or untangling the flags, it's finished. Even though the knot is still there, it's finished.

That's because the Dhamma is here and now. The Dhamma is *akāliko*, timeless, and it's *sandiṭṭhiko*, apparent here and now. The Dhamma doesn't simply happen when the knot is untangled or when the carpet is laid out and all of the food is cooked. It's not, *Okay, the Dhamma is here now, it wasn't here before.* The Dhamma is always here. During the morning reflection, it's here already. The Dhamma doesn't appear just after the reflection is finished, when we begin our practice during the day. It's here now.

If we remember that—really let the mind awaken to that—then that presence to the Dhamma will inform our every action. We can then attune to the *citta*, the heart—to that quality, that fundamental, timeless presence of Dhamma—in the midst of activity. Then any external complications won't contribute to any internal complications, to any internal *papañca*.

So without further ado I offer these thoughts for your consideration today. Enjoy, as they say.

Cows in Good Pasture *

Luang Por Chah's Approach

Luang Por Pasanno • July 2011

Student: I've heard that in the beginning, Luang Por Chah used to lock the doors of the Dhamma hall during the all-night sits.

Luang Por Pasanno: I wasn't there back then. But he did have us sit in meditation right after the meal in all three of our robes—in the hot season! Over time, however, he came to rely more on wisdom than brute force.

Student: What caused him to make this change?

Luang Por Pasanno: Well, he learned that it was better to create the right environment for practice than to try to turn people who didn't want to practice into practitioners. He had a simile. He said: "If you created a nice pasture and cows came in, they would eat the grass. If animals went into the pasture ✓ and didn't eat the grass, then you knew they weren't cows." That was his way of saying that if you create a good place for practice, real practitioners will practice. Other types of people won't practice, and there's no point in trying to change them.

Student: Did he ever provide similes indicating that people can improve?

Luang Por Pasanno: Every simile has a specific point, and it doesn't work outside of that. Ajahn Chah definitely encouraged people and told them they could do it if they tried. They had the teachings, and they were in a good environment. So if they tried, they could succeed.

* The Lord is my shepherd.... "

81

Student: I've heard that he often encouraged people to stay in robes even when they didn't want to.

Luang Por Pasanno: That's right. For instance, there was Ajahn Toon. Every year after the Rains Retreat he would ask Ajahn Chah if he could leave the training, but Ajahn Chah would refuse. This went on for five years. After every Rains Retreat, just like clockwork, there would be Ajahn Toon with his offering of flowers and incense respectfully asking to leave the Saṅgha. Ajahn Chah would always talk him out of it or, sometimes, just get up and walk away. He saw that even though Ajahn Toon wanted to leave, he was capable of persevering in the practice. Ajahn Toon ended up staying a monk, and now he's a really good teacher in our lineage.

A Positive Encounter With Death

Ajahn Yatiko • December 2012

There are many aspects of life that we bring to mind, consciously and repetitively, as part of our training. One focus of our contemplation is on the nature of mortality, the fact that we're all going to die.

I recently had quite a positive experience in this regard. Last night there was a very strong and sharp pain in my chest that lasted several hours. It was running down my arm and the side of my neck and seemed very similar to a heart attack. But I was quite clear that it wasn't a heart attack because the pain felt slightly off to the right rather than to the left where the heart is. During this experience, I found that I could easily pretend and convince myself for a moment that this was a real heart attack.

Physically, it was very painful and difficult to breathe or walk, and I had to sit down for several hours. Interestingly, the earlier part of the day had been quite challenging so that in comparison with that, it actually felt good to suddenly be face-to-face with death. Everything else fell away completely. All the concerns of the day, in a flash, disappeared from my radar.

Two experiences came up quite naturally from this episode. One was a recollection that my life as a monk has been pretty good. Certainly there have been ups and downs, successes and failures, morally and otherwise. But on the whole, I felt ready to die. I thought, *That's okay.* The other experience was having mindfulness throughout the entire episode. I felt that I had stepped outside the body and was observing the situation from above, contemplating what was happening. I was able to see that there was this human body and this process of attachment and reflection. It was a bit surprising. I was looking at the whole situation from this perspective of not-self, and was mindful of that as well.

It was comforting for me to know that it was possible to have this response to the perception of death. Everything that seemed so heavy and weighed me down throughout the day suddenly disappeared like fog on a sunny day. It just vanished.

Clean Kuṭi, Clear Mind

Luang Por Pasanno • May 2013

Keeping our *kuṭis*, our dwelling places, in order helps to keep our minds in order as well. So anytime we leave our kuṭis, we should make sure everything is put away, neat and tidy.

It's easy to let things slide, to tidy up only once a week, or whatever. But if we have a habit of letting things get a bit messy before tidying up, we're apt to develop a somewhat lax attitude about everything, which would make it very difficult to lift up and sustain clarity in meditation. By contrast, when our attitude is to keep things tidy, moment to moment, we're developing the same quality of mind needed to stay with our meditation object, moment to moment, which allows the mind to settle and clarity to arise.

Just as maintaining an orderly kuṭi helps to keeps the dust and dirt from finding places to hide in our living environment, it also promotes the mental qualities needed to expose those places in the mind where the defilements hide away, unobserved. When we're trying to understand the subtleties of the mind, we don't want to have dark corners where the defilements can hide, because they'll tend to hang out there forever. We need to develop habits like this, which assist us in keeping the mind spacious and perceptive. That way, we can see our conditioning, our mental patterns—everything in the mind that creates suffering and discontent.

This mundane task of keeping our kuṭis in order can be extended to our general environment as well. This is a part of our training to make the mind clear, steady, and discerning. When we are consistent with this, these qualities will become part of the mind's normal way of being—its default setting. We won't have to make an effort to lift them up in the mind, because they'll already be there for us, primed and accessible. This in turn will make the mind bright and ready for work.

Cāga: Giving Up

Ajahn Karuṇadhammo • August 2012

I was listening to Ajahn Yatiko give out the work assignments and observing how he adjusted midcourse as he received information about all the people who were or weren't here and who did or didn't do a particular task. It was easy to marvel at the flexibility and ease he conveyed as he juggled around in his mind what was going to take place with the complicated work assignments and multiple tasks.

I remember when I was the work monk for a few months. It wouldn't be impolite to say that it was a disaster. At least that's what it felt like to me. Hearing Ajahn Yatiko just now, I was reflecting on the different ways that people offer themselves and the different skills they have. There is an impulse to give, to serve, to offer oneself to the community in whatever way one can.

During my retreat, I spent some time reflecting on the theme of giving. In the Pāli language there are a couple of different words used for giving. There is *dāna*, which is generosity or giving, and *cāga*, which has a broader scope than generosity. Cāga refers to the aspect of giving as well, but it can be used more with the tone of giving over, giving to something, or giving up in terms of relinquishment. There is a sense of handing over or giving toward some higher ideal that can manifest in many ways. We can give up a material object as an offering with a sense of selflessness. This might be an object we like or something we would like to keep, but for the sake or benefit of somebody else we give it over to someone. With cāga, when we give, it is not with a feeling of loss but rather with a feeling of fulfillment. There is a sense that we are getting more from giving up, from relinquishing, than from holding on.

In our daily lives and in the monastery we give up time to people, give up self-concern, and ask ourselves, *What can I do to make life a little bit easier or a little more pleasant for somebody else?* We may see that someone is overworked or overstretched in what they are doing, and we keep our eyes open for the opportunity to make a gesture of giving. For the residents here, it might mean that we don't go up to our *kuṭis* for another fifteen minutes while we help somebody do something, giving up what we would like to do for the benefit of somebody else.

There is a story from the suttas about three monks who are all practicing well and living harmoniously. When questioned by the Buddha about this, one of the monks explains that his success is due to asking himself, *Why should I not set aside what I wish to do and do what these venerable ones wish to do?*

We can also think about cāga in regard to our views and opinions. This is a monastery with a lot of independent-minded folks, some of whom have strong personalities (I put myself in that category). There can sometimes be a sense that, *I know the best way to do something, therefore that is the way we should do it.* It can be a real workout to notice that inclination, suspend it, and acknowledge that even if we are right, maybe it's not the best way to proceed. There are many collective ways that we do things in the monastery, and even if we don't agree with them, we can acknowledge we have a common agreement to do as the group does and let go of our views and opinions about

the matter. This is what we all signed up for. We operate in ✓
a container, the monastery, that has a fair number of protocols. In this way we give ourselves over to the community in✓
the form of cāga, maintaining harmony even if it means letting
go of some of our views and opinions.

On a more transcendent level, we are giving up and giving over to the Dhamma, relinquishing to the practice and the
training for the realization the Buddha talks about as the end-
point of our practice. Whatever it is that we find we are holding to, clinging to, adhering to, we meet with an attitude of
cāga, of giving up, giving over, and relinquishing. It can be a
formidable task to let go because we often hold onto our old
habits of finding temporary happiness in temporary things. We
give up those tendencies for the benefit of having a long-term
sense of satisfaction and completion. Cāga is one of those qualities that leads to satisfaction, and we can develop it in ways
toward ultimate realization.

A Mango Tree Was My Teacher

Luang Por Pasanno • May 2013

As we practice, one of the qualities that we need to cultivate or attend to is learning how to pay attention to our circumstances, what is happening around us. So often we wait for instruction, the right circumstances, or a sign that we are doing the right thing. For us to really take advantage of the practice, we need to learn from our circumstances and pay attention to the natural processes around us.

There's a story that Ajahn Chah used in his teachings. It is a Jātaka tale about a king who takes his retinue off to do some business. As they pass by an area in the forest, the king sees a wild mango tree full of mangoes and thinks to himself, *Those mangoes look really good. At the end of the day when we're going back to the palace, I'm going to stop by this tree and have some of those mangoes. That will be really refreshing.* Then he moves on. However, the people toward the back of the retinue have a different idea, and they start to bash the tree and shake the tree, knocking the branches down, taking the fallen fruit for themselves.

Evening comes, and the king returns to the same spot. There, before him, is this poor, bashed up, barren tree where he believed all of the mangoes would be hanging. He is disappointed and thinks to himself, *This is really sad. This big tree's been beaten up and abused.* He looks around and sees another mango tree that is not very full and does not have many mangoes on it. Reflecting to himself he thinks, *That tree seems to be the same as it*

90

was before. *There is a real problem with having a full tree, and it's the same problem I have with my life: I have many duties, responsibilities, and many people around me. Maybe I should transform my life to be more like this scrawny mango tree and step out of my worldly duties and responsibilities.* That was his impetus to go forth on the spiritual path to become a religious seeker. In the future, whenever he was asked who his teacher was, he would respond: "A mango tree was my teacher" (Jā 22.60-61).

So when we consider the circumstances, the events, and the natural processes around us, we see that truth is being displayed all the time. The problem is that we don't pay attention, or if we do pay attention, it is not in a way that is reflective—we don't internalize or consider the true meaning. When this happens we don't derive the benefit of the experience; instead, we wait for some kind of overt teaching or instruction. With wise reflection, we learn how to internalize the teachings by observing the events and circumstances around us.

We Don't Have to Struggle

Ajahn Jotipālo • November 2013

Before coming to this practice, most of us had positive ideas about meditation—that it brings peace and happiness, even bliss—and those ideas are what motivated us to become practitioners. For many of us, however, the reality is that meditation can often be a struggle, rather than an experience of bliss and happiness. When we close our eyes, there can be a lot of physical or mental pain. There can be a sense of pushing away from our experiences or a general feeling of discomfort and tension.

When I think about my own practice, what often creates the struggle I experience in meditation is my attitude. I can have an attitude that I'm only meditating to experience peace, not pain. That's a problem. So I can ask myself, *Is it possible to drop that attitude and relax?* If I can drop the attitude, I have the capacity to bring that sense of peace and tranquility into one single moment—the present moment.

Alternatively, when we find we are unable to bear with a particular form of pain, we can also turn our attention away from that pain. If there is pain in the knee, for example, why put our attention on that if our minds cannot hold a sense of steadiness around it? Why bring that into our attention? Instead, we can find some other part of the body that is not in pain so we can experience that feeling of present-moment peace right there.

Ajahn Buddhadāsa used to talk about enlightenment in the sense of experiencing this moment of peace with clarity and then becoming familiar with that experience. Of course it is impermanent, it comes and it goes, but it's a taste. We can train the mind to incline toward that state more and more often, to make it stretch out a little longer, and return to it throughout the day. With training, this experience of peace and clarity can become a touchstone for the mind, and we can turn toward that in meditation when we find ourselves struggling with pain or discomfort.

But the first thing to do when we find ourselves struggling is to remember that we do not have to struggle. Then we can focus on the body or the breath or whatever it is for us that brings that sense of peace and tranquility. Or we can reflect on any one of the seven factors of enlightenment—mindfulness, discernment, energy, rapture, tranquility, concentration, and equanimity—in order to establish a more grounded state of mind.

There are many avenues we can take to cultivate the peace and happiness in meditation that brought many of us to the practice in the first place. Now that we have become committed to the practice, our job is to explore those avenues for ourselves, to discover which ways lead to the most fruitful results.

Which Practice Is Right for Me?

Luang Por Pasanno • April 2013

After the meal today we will be taking formal leave of Ajahn Sucitto. Living as we do in an American Buddhist monastery, we're in a distinct minority and rather isolated. So when visiting teachers like Ajahn Sucitto come here and talk about specific practice experiences they've had, it's a precious opportunity for us. Having listened to them carefully, we can then reflect on our own experience, asking ourselves: *What have I done that works? What has been beneficial? What has helped the mind relinquish its attachments and defilements? What has helped the mind become more peaceful, settled and clear?* It's not something we can learn from a book, reading about some theory and trying to make sense of it. Rather, it's about paying attention to this element of experience—our own experiences and the experiences of others. For instance, when Ajahn Dtun visited here recently, the teachings he offered were always conveyed in terms of his own practice: "This was my experience. This was the practice I used. This is what worked for me." After listening to teachings like that, we may be inspired to apply some of the practices described. But if we do, it's important that we attend to what genuinely works and examine this in our daily lives, interactions, and formal practice.

To put it another way, we can ask ourselves, *What is it that aligns us with Dhamma?* The Buddha tells us that if something aligns or accords with the Dhamma, it's going to increase our happiness, well-being, clarity, and understanding. The opposite is true as well. When what we're doing increases our *dukkha*—our anxieties, confusion, and agitation—it's a pretty sure bet that we're not aligned with the Dhamma. Trying to emulate a practice used by a respected teacher may seem like a fine idea, but the test is whether applying that practice accords with the Dhamma for *you*—in your own, personal experience.

To employ this test skillfully takes practice, reflection, and a willingness to experiment and try things out. But it's something we need to do. Practicing Dhamma in accordance with Dhamma—*dhammānudhamma paṭipatti*—is a quality that needs our close attention. In fact, it's a key element of stream-entry. So as we go about our daily lives, as we continue to cultivate the practice, it is helpful to reflect: *Does what I'm doing accord with Dhamma? What I'm saying, thinking, and feeling—does it accord with Dhamma?* If we are willing to investigate these questions closely, their answers will help us clarify whether our particular practices are leading us in the right direction.

It's important to also understand that what works for us will change, depending on conditions. For instance, just because something worked today doesn't mean it's going to work tomorrow, and what didn't work in the past may work for us now. This makes it necessary for us to adapt and experiment. Often Ajahn Chah would repeat a quote from one of his teachers, Ajahn Tong Rat, who taught that the practice is very straightforward and easy: "If the defilements come high, then duck; if they come low, jump." In other words, we're to do whatever the situation demands—whatever works as long as it is not causing ourselves or others more suffering. This entails first asking ourselves, *How might I work with this particular situation?*

95

Once we have a sense of what might be a good approach, we put it into practice, try it out, and then evaluate the results.

This all points to an ongoing, evolving relationship between the workings of our practice and the workings of our minds. It takes time to discover skillful ways of engaging with that relationship; it's a learning process. But by sticking with this process, by taking a genuine interest in it, we can develop a good sense of what practices—whether from teachers or our own innovations—are truly beneficial, what practices accord with Dhamma, what practices genuinely work for us.

Pūjā for Life

Ajahn Yatiko • June 2012

There's a passage in the suttas in which the Buddha talks about how long people live. He says a person who lives a long life might live 100 years or a bit more. It's interesting that people lived that long in the Buddha's day. According to the suttas, there were many monks who lived to be 80, and a few as old as 120.

Let's assume, for the sake of contemplation, that the longest lifespan since the Buddha's time was 100 years. And let's say that our previous lives were all human. If we lived to be 100 years in each life, it would have been twenty-five lives ago that the Buddha was alive. I think it is helpful to recollect this regularly and make the connection between our own lives and the Buddha's life. We can connect with this remarkable human being who walked the Earth and set rolling the unstoppable wheel of Dhamma. By regularly making this connection to the Buddha, we are consciously bringing to mind this remarkable human being who lived, walked, breathed, and had sense experiences exactly like we do. Whatever we're doing, we can connect it to the Buddha.

Suppose we were to forget about the past, as if the past didn't exist, and imagine that today is the day of our birth, a fresh start. This can inspire us to make a determination to live the rest of our lives as a *pūjā*—as an expression of gratitude to the Buddha: *I want my life to be as well lived, meaningful and beautiful as possible, as a way of honoring the Buddha.*

This morning when we were chanting, I was looking at these beautiful flowers offered to the Buddha and feeling a lot of gratitude arise for the Buddha and what he's done. For many Westerners, the energy of devotion is not easily accessible, but one way to get in touch with it is through this sense of gratitude. If we reflect on what the Buddha did—his awakening to this remarkable and uncompromising Dhamma, his decades of teaching and exemplifying the Dhamma to innumerable beings—we can get a sense of the incredible, meaningful life he led. It can bring up a lot of gratitude, which comes very close to the quality of devotion. Whether we're feeling gratitude or devotion, we can connect it to a sense of doing pūjā for the rest of our lives—for this one lifespan. We could give this life over to the Triple Gem and make the whole practice a pūjā to the Buddha. This is a way of getting outside of ourselves. Sometimes we get caught up with ourselves, thinking, *Is my practice going well? I don't think my meditation is very deep.* We can let all that go when we're connected to the quality of pūjā.

We can take the next twenty, thirty, or forty years—whatever we possibly have left—and make our lives an offering to the Buddha. We could do everything as an expression of our gratitude. It's not an empty gesture where we think, *I haven't realized anything significant from my practice so I might as well give it to the Buddha.* It's not like that at all. It's a refined and beautiful practice in and of itself. We can turn it into a whole meditation; we can use our whole day simply reflecting on this. Suddenly, we might find ourselves happily cleaning our shrine, no longer holding the attitude that, *I'll clean my shrine, but only because it's monastery etiquette.* It's more like it is an expression of our practice, because the highest pūjā we can offer is to be mindful of the present moment and contemplate our experience. That's really what pūjā is about. If we think in this way, pūjā becomes a very valuable practice and is quite nourishing to our hearts.

Developing Samaṇa Saññā

Luang Por Pasanno • July 2005

Yesterday, at the City of the Dharma Realm in Sacramento, I was giving instructions to twenty-eight novices who were preparing to ordain next month as *bhikṣunīs*, Buddhist nuns. It was quite a delightful time. Their sincerity was tangible.

One of the ideas I brought up with them is developing *samaṇa saññā*, the perception or recollection of being a religious seeker. We function out of our perceptions. We perceive something to be interesting or desirable, and we get excited. We perceive something to be worrisome or troublesome, and we start to have aversion or negativity. Perceptions are always informing how we relate to things. The Buddha encouraged us to develop the perception or recollection of being religious seekers. In that way, we can relate to the circumstances we find ourselves in and to the people we live with from a very different perspective. By perceiving ourselves to be religious seekers—those who are seeking peace—we encourage ourselves to always relate and act in the best possible manner.

So how do we conduct ourselves? What do we do as seekers? How do we engage in our responsibilities and duties in order to maintain a quality of peace? How do we fulfill that aspiration? We do this by reminding ourselves and recollecting, *Yes, this is what I am, this is what I'm doing and most valuable for me to be doing—seeking peace, seeking truth.*

As we take on duties or have contact and engagement with each other, we can relate to each other as fellow seekers of truth and peace, rather than as objects of aversion, attention, or interest, or just somebody else who can fulfill a function. There are times when we may think, *There's the person who does the computer work. There's the person who is the kitchen manager. There's the person who does this or that.* We might see that person only in a particular role or having a certain type of personality. This really limits us and limits everybody else as well.

Instead, we can recollect ourselves as samaṇas and develop a perception of each other as fellow seekers of peace, fellow seekers of truth. This helps us support our own practice, our own daily living in a way that is peaceful and encourages us to live skillful lives in the monastery.

Our Collective Going Forth

Ajahn Amaro • October 2008

This is a big day for Venerable Kaccāna. After arriving at Abhayagiri about two and a half years ago, today he is making the commitment to ordain and go forth into the *Bhikkhu Saṅgha* and is taking on the precepts of training. It's helpful during occasions like this to reflect on the process of going forth into the Saṅgha—*upasampadā*—which means lifted or raised up. It not only reflects an outer process, but an inner process as well. It's the formal commitment of an individual to this particular training and his acceptance into the group of monks. It also reflects an inner commitment and an inner change that's useful for us to consider, whether we have hair and wear trousers or have a shaved head and wear a robe.

Essentially when we talk about ordaining, it's usually in terms of going forth from the household life into homelessness, from being an *agārika* to an *anagārika*, one who lets go of the household life. But in many ways, it's more about going forth from self-centered thinking to seeing in terms of Dhamma. It's going forth from confusion to clarity, from a life of being half awake or not awake at all to wakefulness. That's something that is useful for all of us to reflect on whether we're living as a lay practitioner with commitments and responsibilities in the world, as an anagārika, as a *sāmaṇera*, or as a *bhikkhu* who has already ordained. If we've formally made the commitment, have been "raised up" into the Saṅgha, and have already gone forth, still, the most important aspect of what we are doing is that going forth from confusion and self-centered thinking to being awake. Unfortunately, we sometimes hang on to the formal commitment of having gone forth and taking the precepts of a monk so that after years of experience, we can forget the part about waking up, about going forth from confusion to clarity and seeing in terms of Dhamma.

Whether we're a lay person or a monastic, this auspicious day of Sāmaṇera Kaccāna's going forth can encourage all of us to go forth in terms of our attitudes, the way that we relate to the world. We can choose to be mindful, to be awake, and to be not so self-concerned or self-obsessed.

On a practical level we have many tasks to pull together today in preparation for the ordination. But, it's good to bear in mind these reflections, not just as a philosophical aspiration, but also in terms of how we work with each other. We can bring that quality of mindfulness and self-relinquishment to the work we're doing—to our concerns, the tasks we have, and the way we relate to other people. Whether carrying a cumbersome bench through the forest, maneuvering a ladder, or setting up the ordination platform, we're bringing that quality of wakefulness and attentiveness to the time and place of the situation and the way we're functioning with each other. That quality of attentiveness will then inform all of our tasks so that the day itself becomes a resonance of the gesture of going forth. That's what the ceremony is all about. In this way it really makes going forth alive and meaningful, informing all of our lives. It's not only helping outside, it's also helping us to work on our inner lives, our inner worlds. In this way it is our collective going forth.

Our Changing Bodies

Ajahn Karuṇadhammo • September 2012

Some people here have recently experienced the death of someone close to them. Also, a number of the community members here have experienced minor injuries to joints, feet, and knees, as well as other illnesses and maladies. When we reflect on the nature of our human bodies, we can see these bodies aren't really under our control. They don't obey our wishes, our wants, or our desires to be healthy and always comfortable. They have their own quirks. Each one of our bodies has a particular set of constituents, elements, and predispositions through kamma, biology, and genetics. Each body is more or less following its own life, its own course, and there is not a huge amount of control that we have over it. We can try to influence it and try to give it proper nourishment and support when we are ill, but by and large there is nothing we can do to control its ultimate outcome. It will age. Along the way, it will experience periods of health, periods of sickness, and eventually the body will die. It is simply a part of nature. That's the way nature works.

Look around at what is happening with plants and animals. All creatures have their birth, their time of life, and their passing away. It's so easy to get caught up in this process, to get caught up in the fear of illness or injury. There can often be a lot of anxiety about how we protect and care for the human body, not to mention the fear, anxiety, and difficulties we experience from the death and dying process.

The hallmark of the Buddha's practice is to contemplate this reality so that we can genuinely see, understand, and accept that it's all simply a part of nature. If we look around we can see that there's nothing that escapes this process. Gently, over time, we can apply this contemplation to ourselves and to what we experience throughout the day. By gaining insight into this process, we are able to live without a constant sense of protection and anxiety in regard to this body, which is merely following its own course. We look after ourselves in reasonable ways but without attachment or clinging to a sense that, *This is who I am; this is myself.* The body is basically a set of elements that is constantly changing, moving, evolving, and transforming, just like the world around us.

Only Part of the Picture

Luang Por Pasanno • May 2012

As we did with conducting the recent ordination—thinking through things a bit, planning a little—we're developing a sense of circumspection as we attend to whatever circumstances we're in. We do this by asking ourselves, *How can I fit into this situation? How can I be skillful, effective, and composed?* Sometimes people can misunderstand how to apply the Buddha's teachings on being present in the moment, and they may think, *All I need to do is be present in this moment, and everything will be okay.* But that's only part of the picture.

The Buddha always encouraged his followers to recognize and pay attention to the causal nature of actions. What we've done in the past affects the present, and what we're doing in the present affects the future. Having seen and understood how those principles play out over time, we shape our behavior accordingly.

Sometimes there's an emphasis on having a nice, warm and fuzzy, be-here-now kind of feeling. But in reality, when people are guided by that sort of feeling, they're usually not very well connected with themselves or the circumstances around them. The Buddha didn't advocate that. Instead, he encouraged us to learn how to connect with the world skillfully. So we practice being attentive and effective with our tasks, duties, and interactions with other people.

When we learn to do that, we can build a firm foundation of clarity and clear comprehension—*sampajañña*. The Buddha spoke of sampajañña as clearly comprehending the circumstances we're in, the people we're with, and the effects we're having on the world around us. With this quality we can anchor our actions in our own non-delusion, non-confusion. And when we apply sampajañña to our present-moment circumstances, it allows us to see a much bigger picture.

Using the Communal Life Skillfully

Ajahn Yatiko • August 2013

At one point while we were meditating together this morning, I became vividly aware of the silence. Suddenly, it became extremely still, and I had a very strong sense of collective practice, a sense of shared activity with fellow practitioners. It was a very beautiful moment. I think religious groups in general provide a sense of community or family, because people in those communities spend so much time with each other, in mutual care and support. That's very meaningful and valuable.

At the same time, living in community can mask the truth of our own aloneness. When it comes time to die, we die alone. The people around us when we die, with all their good wishes and best intentions, still continue to live their own lives and deal with their daily tasks. I imagine that in many cases this fact is not fully apparent to those who are dying. They might be lying there wondering, *Doesn't anybody realize this is happening to me, that I'm leaving soon?* They're not fully in touch with the natural fact that life goes on, whether it includes them or not. We are born alone; we die alone. Moreover, even while we are alive and have many close relationships, it is inevitable that those relationships will end eventually, one way or another. Perhaps a long-term friend disrobes, or our teacher disrobes or dies, or a partner or family member leaves us or dies. This experience is very painful for many people, but we are subject to having that experience at any time. That's a truth that living in community can mask.

Despite this truth, living in community can serve as a useful crutch. Our existential situation can be compared to a person who breaks a leg; while the leg is healing, there's a need for physical support, like a pair of crutches. In this respect, religious institutions and relationships are like crutches. This is not a value judgment, it's simply a fact and a recognition that crutches are important for people in need of support. In a community, we live in the presence of other people. We have the responsibility to care for them. We provide them with crutches, and they do the same for us when the need arises. And when we help others, it lessens our self-centeredness and our unhealthy sense of self-importance. That's good for us and good for others. Everyone wins.

With the loss of friends, we can be reminded of our own existential aloneness. At the same time, we can remember the support we receive in community. We can remember that when people leave us, the community will encourage us to take our loss in the spirit of letting go, rather than encouraging us to tightly grasp our crutches, hoping we'll never be without them. Crutches are not supposed to be around forever. Their purpose is to assist and lend strength until they are no longer needed. So we care for ourselves, care for each other, and care for the community in which we live, while recalling and respecting the fact of our aloneness.

Caring for Everything We Use

Luang Por Pasanno • June 2005

Throughout the day it is helpful for us to recollect that we are a community of alms mendicants. We rely on what is offered to us as gifts of goodwill: robes, alms food, shelter, and medicine—the four requisites. Traditionally, in Thai monasteries, the monastic community brings the requisites to mind as part of its formal morning and evening chanting. The chants encourage the monastics to ask themselves, *Did I use the requisites skillfully? Was I heedful when I used them? Do I understand their true purpose?* We too should reflect in this way. It's easy to expect that everything will be there for us and that everything will be of good quality. But as alms mendicants, the emphasis is on contentment with what we have and being circumspect with what we are using.

There's a story about a monk who was cleaning Ajahn Maha Boowa's *kuṭi* and threw away two used matches that were on the altar. When the Ajahn returned to his room, he asked his attendant, "What happened to those matches? They weren't used up yet!" It was Ajahn Maha Boowa's habit to use partially burnt matches for transferring the flame from one candle to another candle or to other objects; he wouldn't dispose of a match until it was completely burnt out. This example can inspire us to develop a sense of using things fully. The focus is not on our convenience, but on recollecting that these things are offerings; they have value, and we shouldn't waste them.

110

Another aspect of our relationship with material things has to do with respect and compassion for others in the community. It's really basic: make sure that people don't have to pick up or clean up after you. Return things to their proper place. After using a tool, put it back where it belongs, rather than leaving it out for someone else to put away. In the kitchen, putting a used dish in the sink doesn't magically make it clean and placed back in the cupboard. A real human being has to do that. We show respect and compassion for others by being considerate.

Beyond that, take responsibility for setting things right, even if they are not your assigned responsibility. If you see that something is out of place or hasn't been done, don't just walk by and leave it for someone else. Take the responsibility and initiative to be helpful. If everybody learns to take responsibility in this way, then it's not a burden for anyone.

Whether we are in the monastery or elsewhere, we rely on the requisites and other material items for our daily existence. Looking after these things is just an aspect of mindfulness—attending to what we're doing and what needs to be done in the present moment. This is not so mundane that we don't need to think about it. We learn to incorporate the way we care for material requisites into our day-to-day practice of mindfulness and cultivation of skillful qualities. The material realm will then become a more harmonious and pleasant place in which to live.

Reflecting on Interdependence

Ajahn Karuṇadhammo • July 2013

In recent years there's been a modern Western interpretation of dependent co-arising that's derived from an explanation of the interdependence in the world, with the people in it being interconnected in a vast web of cause-and-effect relationships and experience—"It's all connected," as people like to say. There's a belief that there's no type of action or activity in the world that doesn't have some sort of effect on the whole of existence, all action and interaction. This isn't a very accurate representation of what the Buddha's teaching on dependent origination is all about. It's actually pretty far from what the Buddha taught. Dependent origination is a teaching about how ignorance conditions the arising of suffering and all the various factors involved, as well as the cessation of that entire process.

Nevertheless, the idea of interdependence is something that can be helpful to contemplate, because even though it may not be valid in terms of dependent origination, it has a truth to it. We're very much affected by each other, dependent on each other, and influence each other, and we're inexplicably woven together through the various forces of kamma in our cyclical existence in saṃsāra. With this, there are all the various ways that kamma works itself out that we don't really understand and can't possibly comprehend because it's so complicated. We find ourselves weaving through many, many lifetimes, receiving the results of our past actions, being involved with each other over and over again, and bound together in our commonality as beings coursing through saṃsāra.

We don't know exactly how that process works, but it is possible to understand that each of our rebirths in saṃsāra depends on our relationships with other people and, for better or for worse, how we respond to situations and the qualities we develop in relationship to each other. Due to causes and conditions, skillful actions and intentions that have been put in place by us in our past lives, by some fortunate set of incredible circumstances—some might call it a miracle—we find ourselves existing in the same space and time, right here and now, practicing with each other in this vast web of existence. So we need to ask ourselves, *How well am I spending my time?*

I think it's important to reflect on that because it points out how much we need to rise up to this circumstance we find ourselves in and take responsibility for what we are doing right now, acknowledging what it's taken for us to get here and not wasting this precious opportunity. It's so unusual for us to all be here together with a strong interest in practicing the Dhamma—it's not a widespread inclination that's happening in the world. Perhaps there are small pockets of it here or there but by and large it's an incredibly rare opportunity. We can do our best to take full advantage of this situation because this life is short, and we don't know exactly where we're going to end up the next time around. We keep the momentum going by cultivating the wholesome and skillful qualities we want to bring with us. These qualities carry on into the future in case we don't finish our work in this lifetime.

All of the wholesome intentions we cultivate now will condition what happens for us the next time around and, most importantly, will condition the quality of our lives right here and right now. We are working on letting go of unskillful tendencies: aversion, greed, self-interest, and selfishness, and we are cultivating qualities of virtue and generosity, to make a commitment to ending the cycle of suffering. That's how we can increase the potential of being in association with like-minded people in lifetimes to come. This is the meaning of true interdependence.

Is Rock Climbing Like Meditation?

Luang Por Pasanno • June 2013

As Dhamma practitioners, we need to continually turn our attention to contemplation, reflection, investigation—to consider things carefully—and not just in formal meditation, but also as we go about our more mundane activities. These days, even in the mainstream media, it's popular to talk about "being in the present moment, being in the here and now." It sounds very good, but if that's all we practice, we can be left without having reflected or investigated to any great degree.

We need to apply some discernment. When we experience difficulty, conflict, or dis-ease, we direct our attention toward that, investigate its causes, and examine the process by which it is unfolding. This is not to say we should be reaching out intellectually and coming up with rational explanations; rather, it is being willing to investigate and bring one's attention to the matter at hand.

Once when Ajahn Chah was visiting the U.S. someone asked him a question about the need for sitting meditation: "I have a friend whose meditation is rock climbing. He doesn't have to sit in meditation to concentrate his mind. Why do we have to sit in meditation? Couldn't we do something like rock climbing—anything that puts us in the present moment?" Then Ajahn Chah asked him, "When your friend is rock climbing, does he contemplate the Four Noble Truths?"

We can be in the present moment, we can be clear, but are we developing discernment and learning to understand the nature of the mind, the nature of conditions? We mustn't be satisfied with merely cultivating calm and clarity; rather, that calm and clarity needs to be put to work. Its work is developing discernment and understanding. That's the crux of our practice. Take the illuminating idiom, "truth-discerning awareness." It's not just about awareness—it's awareness with discernment.

To develop this discernment we can begin by asking ourselves, *What is the nature of things—the nature of conditions—the nature of my own mind?* Then we bring the attention inward and focus our awareness on the various feelings that are present. In particular, we attend to the feelings of dis-ease, dissatisfaction, or suffering and come to understand that those feelings are merely feelings. With any particular feeling we have, we ask ourselves, *What are the causal conditions for that feeling? Where is its resolution? How can I help bring about that resolution?* In this way, we are contemplating the Four Noble Truths exactly as the Buddha intended.

Mindfulness With Moods and Defilements

Ajahn Yatiko • June 2013

Ajahn Chah once said that if we have three seconds without mindfulness, it's like three seconds of madness. Without mindfulness we can get lost in moods—happiness, despair, depression, elation, whatever. Mindfulness is not about getting rid of our moods. It's about being able to observe them clearly, to step back from them and recognize, *This is simply what I'm experiencing.* It's being able to see moods as a flow, like clouds moving through the sky.

During group meditation, it can appear as if nobody is experiencing a mood except us; everyone else is sitting there with faces that seem to look bored, while we're trying to be with some intense emotion. This is an experience some of us have. Others among us don't have a lot of emotional content or aren't really aware of it. Some people can be very much in their heads and quite rational, absorbed in thought, analysis, or speculation. Others can be absorbed in some mood, positive or negative. But mindfulness is that which is in the background, containing all of those experiences.

That's what we want to cultivate—that capacity to observe whatever it is we're experiencing. To be able to watch our experiences, moods, biases, rationalizations, and justifications is one of the most important skills that we can develop as practitioners. This process is connected with recognizing and accepting who we are. We're all doing our best in a monastery. We don't have to be anything we're not.

On the other hand, we also need to question ourselves about how a defilement manifests and to recognize when a defilement has arisen in the mind. When a defilement *has* arisen, it's unhelpful to rationalize or justify it. The defilements are not going to disappear on their own. They are something we look at, recognize, and see clearly. We try to understand how these defilements are leading to suffering. Attaching to our desires, justifying, rationalizing, insisting on, and following our defilements all lead to suffering. Mindfulness is that which leads us out of suffering.

So whether we're investigating our moods or working with the defilements, mindfulness is the key. It's what replaces madness with sanity.

Everything Is Mind-Attended

Ajahn Amaro • December 2008

Even though the snow falls nearly every year, I'm always struck by the same impression: how much it changes the perception of the world I live in. Water arriving in a particular form, turning all the horizontal and semi-horizontal surfaces white, the sound and the shape, everything highlighted in a strange, unusual way, all the color washed out. It's a very good teaching, isn't it?

It's like the mood of the mind. It can be so persistent when it's stuck on some track, excited, irritated, or worried about something. There seems to be a coloring of the whole world. *This is my problem. I'm supposed to worry about this. I have to worry about this. This is my project. The only thing that really matters in the world is fixing the railings at the Bhikkhu Commons or clearing the trap under the sink at Casa Serena.* The center of the world is this particular job we have, these letters that have to be written, or this meal that has to be cooked. These things that the mind latches onto seem so real and permanent—our particular projects, responsibilities, fears, hopes, and desires. *Well, of course it's that way. Can't you see?* Then suddenly—snap! Overnight the world changes color, and there's a whole different mood. Suddenly, *Oh look, it's all different.* How utterly transformed our perceptions can be when there is simply a different shape, coloring of the landscape, or sound of the valley.

119

This is an excellent reflection on our moods. When we think we're in the middle of some difficult tangle, some big issue or conflict, an important project, a difficult relationship—suddenly it all shifts. Poof! It's not a problem anymore because it just changed. The thing that we thought we had to worry about wasn't anything we needed to be concerned about in the first place. It wasn't the way we thought it was. It was a mistaken impression. When we see and reflect in this way—how much the world can change when we're in the midst of some particular anxiety, worry, project, or activity—it helps to provide a perspective. *Oh, this is only my impression. Now I see.*

We get caught up in thinking, *I have my name written on this particular issue. It's mine. I'm responsible for this project. I have to dig this hole. I have to fix this railing. I'm the one who has to pay the debt.* It seems so real and important, so much like it's the center of the world. We see what the mind has put onto it, what Luang Por Chah would call "a mind-attended thing." He would say, "Everything is mind attended." Even though in the Abhidhamma it says there are some things which are mind-attended and there are some things which are not mind-attended, Luang Por Chah would say, "Well, actually, everything is mind-attended." As soon as we know about something, we form an opinion, make a judgment, and create things with our thoughts.

A simple event like a snowfall, a change of the landscape, and we're reminded that this particular thing that's so significant to us is only significant because of our particular conditioning, our particular expectations, fears, hopes, or abilities. The thing's significance is not inherent, it's merely something the mind has added onto the thing. With this realization we can carry out the work we need to do. We can fix those railings, dig this hole, cook that food, answer those letters, and move that table around those difficult corners in a much more easeful and peaceful way. It's not the center of the world. We can see that it isn't so personal, so burdensome, or so much about "me" and "mine." When we realize this, then everything we need to attend to—the events of the day and the responsibilities that we have—is much more natural and easy to carry out. It becomes more like breathing. The body does it on its own. It doesn't have to be "me" or the ego that does it. Gravity works on its own—I don't have to *do* gravity. When we start to function with that same kind of naturalness and easefulness, working and living in community becomes just like breathing.

A Superior Resolve

Luang Por Pasanno • August 2013

Yesterday, four senior monks from Abhayagiri participated in the ordination at the City of Ten Thousand Buddhas. The preceptor was Reverend Heng Sure. As he was instructing the candidates, he kept using a certain refrain: "There is inferior resolve, medium resolve, and superior resolve." The examples he gave of inferior and medium resolve were humorous, so as to encourage the prospective monks to take on superior resolve.

It's helpful to reflect on what it means to make a resolution and to understand that the way we resolve to do something is going to condition the result. Whether it's about ordaining or simply helping with the dishes, we're constantly resolving to undertake specific activities. We set up in our minds a firm resolve to do the thing we want done, and then pay attention to the result that resolve has on our actions. When we don't do that, the mind tends to wander, drift, and get lost and scattered; we forget about our resolve to stick with whatever it is that we're doing.

It is important to develop the ability of attending to and following through on our resolutions. That's because, after setting a resolution with a particular activity, we often find ourselves experiencing restlessness or boredom when actually engaged in that activity—whether it's meditation or some mundane task. When that happens, we end up replacing what we're doing with something else, and the cycle begins again.

There's the idiom that nature abhors a vacuum. When we leave a vacuum in the mind, it tends to fill up with habits that aren't very useful. We can help prevent that from happening by filling the vacuum with the sense of resolve. We can bring up specific resolutions and follow through on them. We can investigate the very nature of resolutions, asking ourselves, *What am I undertaking? Why am I undertaking it? What are the results of my intentions?*

In essence, we are resolving to take an interest in what we are doing—to be interested in the process of being present and applying ourselves to the activities at hand. That kind of resolve allows the mind to be buoyant and uplifted. If we sustain this practice, the mind will become easily settled and clear. It's all about learning to bring about superior resolve and holding that resolve with understanding and discernment.

This Is the Dissolving

Ajahn Sucitto • May 2007

What if I get it wrong? What if it doesn't work? What if I'm left here alone?

Just look over the edge of that "what if." Let your mind open up and realize that you've been running away from phantoms. Examine the attitudes you might have like, *What if I get it wrong?* We've been getting it wrong all our life—it's no big deal! Everybody's making mistakes and losing it. We've all been blundering, not noticing, disrespectful, impolite, unkind. We've been talking too long or not saying enough. Everybody's getting it wrong. Why don't we just practice forgiveness instead and get out of this trap? You forgive me, and I'll forgive you, okay?

Yes, everything is breaking down. But we can get through that, we can be bigger than that. We can be bigger than getting it right and wrong. We can be bigger than success and failure, praise and blame, gain and loss. What a relief to get out of the game. There will be some pain, though, and we might even cause pain. Maybe the way out of it is being a bit more relaxed, at ease, broad-minded, and less concerned about being right, perfect, on time, prepared, well-defended, and approved.

We can go down into our bellies, relax, breathe out, open up, and trust that as human beings we have what it takes to *be* human beings. We can learn from that process, and we can learn to not make a big deal out of it. We can learn to not get

124

confused by it or expect miracles out of it. Then we can learn to let go of it, to come out of it—and to come out of the agitation and self-consciousness that arises up in these forms.

This is important to learn, isn't it? It is nothing esoteric or high-minded, just basic sanity. But the wonderful thing is that, although it is very ordinary, it is also extremely profound because it starts to dismantle all those reflexes that seem so ingrained and out of control—reflexes that grip us, push us around, make us flustered, say things we wish we hadn't said, or make us feel bad.

We can simply start to dismantle all that stuff, to dismantle our hold on all that need—the need to be something, prove something, get somewhere—until we can be, miraculously, right here, in a place that doesn't have a location. Because it doesn't have a location, we never leave it. Because we never leave it, we *can't* leave it. So there isn't any kind of grief or sadness, up or down, holding on, or worrying.

In the ongoing truthfulness of our practice it's important to sift through all the static and white noise that the emotions and the mind's programs set up. It's important to see and get a handle on what intention feels like in our nervous system. And the same with the quality of attention—to see how big, narrow, tight, or bound we feel when we're occupied with a series of thoughts—how our attention bunches up with that sort of proliferation. We start to get a real sense of how this feels in the body. Then we start to get a sense of what it's like to release it all.

This is what we practice. This is the dissolving. Dissolving involves letting go of control, self-image, and self-territories. For that to happen, it has to be a comfortable ride. We can feel that comfort in the breathing in and the breathing out, in good friendship, and in moral living. We get the sense that *It's okay. It's okay to be here.* That gives us the ability to trust the process and to trust the practice.

Applying Effort Before Death

Luang Por Pasanno • July 2005

One of the American monks in Thailand, Tan Paññāvuḍḍho, has just died. He had been spending the Rains Retreat at Ajahn Dtun's monastery. Yesterday morning, he didn't show up for alms round. A monk was sent to check on him, and he was found lifeless in the bathroom. It looked like he fainted while standing up, fell, and hit his head on the way down.

We remind ourselves of these concepts: *I am of the nature to age, I have not gone beyond aging; I am of the nature to sicken, I have not gone beyond sickness; I am of the nature to die, I have not gone beyond dying.* We may think these concepts apply to sometime in the future—somewhere else, not now—but that is not the case. We carry old age, sickness, and death with us all the time. Something that is very mundane and we do all the time, such as getting up at night to go to the toilet—well, tonight may be the last time for us to do that. It's always important to recollect and remember that, making sure we are using our time skillfully. Tan Paññāvuḍḍho was a very diligent and sincere monk. He had a career track waiting for him in the world but chose not to take it. Instead, he became a monk, used his time skillfully, and put effort into his spiritual life.

However long we have to live, it is so important to put effort into that which is skillful, directing our effort toward the deathless. This can have an extraordinary benefit, not only for us, but for everyone else. The effort we put into disentangling ourselves from *saṃsāra*—cyclical rebirth—is of immense benefit. Saṃsāra keeps weaving its entangling web because of the inappropriate effort we make buying into it. However, by looking at the realities of the human condition, we can apply appropriate effort to free ourselves from saṃsāra, and do that which is of the most benefit for our lives.

Toward a Reliable Refuge

Ajahn Yatiko • December 2012

This morning was one of those times for me when meditation went quite well and was peaceful and bright. At the same time, I kept reminding myself that there's no condition, even in meditation, that can be a refuge. The same goes for life in general. It's good to contemplate that fact during our meditation. While attending to our bodies, feelings, and everything that's arising, we can say to ourselves, *Nope, this is not a refuge.* When we do this, we find that our fear softens. There's nothing to fear, because there is no condition that is a problem. Neither the condition nor the fear is us. We don't get stuck on anything because we've separated ourselves from the problem, relaxing and stepping back.

The mind can obsess about different subjects—for example, the electrical system in the monastery. When we reflect that the electrical system or thoughts about it are not a refuge, then the mind can let go of obsessing about that and step back from it. The electrical system doesn't really matter. We are going to be dead soon, and in the bigger picture it doesn't matter how the electrical system is functioning.

This is the same with whatever mood we are experiencing. Moods are an obstacle to our practice, because we're so tempted to believe in them. With a dark, despairing, frustrated mood, or a bright, blissful, joyful mood—it doesn't matter which—consciousness can get stuck on the perception or belief either way. More to the point, moods can't provide a reliable refuge—they come and go like the wind.

We should contemplate our experiences and remind ourselves: when moods are good, that's not a refuge; when moods are bad, that's not something to get stuck on. Since everything we experience, feel, and imagine is moving and transient, this particular practice may help us understand that none of these things can be taken as a true refuge. The refuge lies elsewhere. So we go through this process of deconstructing our experiences, stepping back from these experiences, and that's the way we move toward a reliable refuge.

Whose Is This?

Ajahn Karuṇadhammo • August 2013

A few days ago I noticed that just above the door of my *kuṭi*, there is a large colony of yellow jackets that has decided to make its home under my roof. Yellow jackets are notoriously territorial. As the summer continues on and becomes hotter and drier, there is less food and as the colony size grows the wasps tend to get more and more aggressive. I have been stung by yellow jackets in the past, and their stings can be pretty painful. Given these circumstances I knew that I needed to take care of the situation. The first thoughts that went through my mind when I initially saw them were: *They are in my kuṭi. This is my kuṭi, and they shouldn't be here. I need to do something to get them out.*

I tried to figure out a way to do that so that they would be deterred, but not harmed. I thought I could accomplish this by spraying them with water, albeit from a good distance. It seemed to me that would aggravate them enough so they would leave their nest long enough for me to take it down and move it further away. I've sprayed them a number of times over the past few days and it does, indeed, stir them up. In fact, a couple of them have found me more than twenty feet away, and I've been stung twice. After the first couple of days observing them in their territorial and protective nature, I was reminded of how really foolish it is to have any sense of ownership around *my kuṭi*. It's likely that their sense of possession is even stronger than mine, to the point of aggressively defending their position. For them it is *their kuṭi,* not mine, and they are simply defending their territory against me. This is another reminder of the sense of ownership and control we have, the sense we have of being the center of experience and generally the center of the universe. We tend to carry this sense around with us most of the time.

So it's beneficial to pose these questions to ourselves: *To whom does this belong? To whom does this kuṭi belong? To whom does this monastery belong?* The other night in Vinaya class we were talking about the ownership of property, especially as it pertains to monks. We say the Abhayagiri Monastic Corporation owns the property of the monastery. Well, does it really? What about all the other beings that exist in the buildings? They probably have a sense that they own the whole monastery.

This feeling of ownership also extends to all of the things that give us a sense of who we are, particularly the human body. We tend to think of this body as *my body, my foot, my knee, my back,* and do what is necessary to defend ourselves against all of the situations that might come and threaten the body. We treat illnesses, and we take care of whatever has befallen us with a sense of possession, a sense that this has happened to *my body.* We take antibiotics or put on different ointments and salves to defend the body against all of the organisms that are taking over. But the millions of organisms that live in our bodies may think of these bodies as theirs (if they do think). It's helpful to ask ourselves: *Whose body is this? Whose feelings are these? Whose thoughts are these? Whose opinions are these? Whose neuroses are these? Whose problems are these?* We have such a strong sense of ownership around all of this. We hope to do whatever is possible to reasonably maximize comfort and skillfulness, yet, if we have a sense of personal attachment, personal identity, to any of this, then at some point when things change, we are bound to suffer.

This is a reflection we can keep in mind as we practice throughout the day. Even though we spend a lot of time developing skillful means and use a fair amount of intention and will, we need to ask ourselves, *Who is in charge? Whose is this? To whom does this all belong?* We don't have to come to any specific logical conclusions. These questions are asked to open up a space for uncertainty, and they help us see our bodies as changing phenomena over which we truly do not have any ultimate control.

Escaping the Infinite Rut

Ajahn Amaro • August 2008

We begin another day, reflecting on the tasks that we all have, the lists of things to do, the never-ending need to attend to the kitchen, the various work projects, guest-monk duties, construction, and so forth. There's a sense of continuity, of things carrying on from where we were before, going on and on. Ajahn Chah once came up with a wonderful simile: "*Saṃsāra* is like the ruts left behind the wheels of a cart. As the wheels turn, the trail that's left behind them goes on and on." There's a sense of repetition, a continuous extension through time. But the wheel itself is very stable, it simply pivots around its axle. Even though the wheel is finite in length, it leaves an infinite trail behind it.

Often we can focus on the infinite trail of the things we've done or need to do. We get caught up by the sense of past and future, endlessly stretching out behind and before us. But the essential aspect is that one point where the wheel meets the ground. If we establish a quality of real attention, then that's all there is. It's simply this one moment as the edge of the wheel meets the ground, this one particular space of experience, this place where we know the qualities of sight, sound, smell, taste, touch, memory, and planning. It all happens here, in this moment, in the space of this mind. *Right now, I'm sitting here, listening to these words of the Ajahn, having tea in silence, the weight of the body on the ground, feelings of coolness, warmth, tiredness.* It's all happening here in the space of our awareness. This is the wheel meeting the ground. There's a quality of great simplicity, stillness, and stability to this.

So even though there's a dynamism, a flow of experience, and perceptions come and go, there's also a quality of stillness. Luang Por Chah phrased it well: "It's like still, flowing water." The mind that is aware and knows is still, but the perceptions, thoughts, feelings, memories, ideas, and plans have a quality of flowing, of continually and unrelentingly moving. It's so easy for us to be caught up in the urgencies of what's gone before or what we have to do, and then to create a sense of self around that in the present moment. It's important to question this process. When the urgencies of the mind come up—*I did this, and I have to do that, and I need to get this done, and so-and-so is going to call, I have to, I have to*—it's good to get out of the rut, as it were, to stop obsessing on the "have done's" and the "have to's," and question the feeling of urgency, obligation, and entanglement with past and future. We can ask ourselves, *Is this endless trail of doing and being done the whole story? Is this the only way to perceive things?* In this way, we can challenge our presumptuous habits of judging the past, judging the future, and judging the present. *Is that so? Is that really the case? Is that the whole story? Oh, it's good.—Is that so? Oh, it's terrible.—Really? Is that so?*

Practicing the Dhamma doesn't take much. It doesn't take a lot of complicated activity, but it does take application. It takes remembrance, recollection, and mindfulness—*sati*. The word *sati* means remembering to pay attention. If we don't remember, if we don't bring attention to the practice, then that shift of perspective—escaping the rut of past and future—doesn't happen. But if we do remember, then we're able to bring to mind the quality of recollection. *What's the hurry? Where do I think I'm* going? *Oh, is that so? This is great; this is terrible. Is that really so?* It only takes the tiniest suggestion, the briefest recollection, to catalyze that realization in the heart: *Of course, how did I believe that was the whole story? Oh right, it's just a judgment. It's merely a perception. It's only a plan.*

The Dedication of Merit and Blessings

Luang Por Pasanno • May 2013

The dedication of merit and blessings is a practice that is very common and ordinary in Buddhist cultures like Thailand. This practice helps counteract our tendency to focus on the problems, the flaws, and the obstacles we believe we have to overcome, whether real or perceived. We can set all that aside and instead, bring our attention to the conditions in our lives that are blessings—those conditions that align themselves with what is meritorious and good.

It's not so difficult to do. If we think of the surroundings we're in—they're about as idyllic as we could hope for. We're not oppressed by war, famine, or pestilence. It's an incredibly fortunate time and place we live in. These are blessings. And while we are under government regulation with our building codes and other mundane details, the government doesn't prohibit monasteries like ours from existing. So we have this opportunity to live here in an American Buddhist monastery, and to practice the Dhamma.

In addition, there are so many people who freely offer their support to us. We have more than adequate food, dwelling places, clothing, and medicine. We're supported every day by people's generosity, and we live in dependence on them. It's essential for us to recollect that truth—that blessing—and by frequently practicing the dedication of blessings to others, we can keep that recollection fresh in our minds.

As monastics, we are not only on the receiving end. It's also our role to give and to share. In carrying out this role, we have the opportunity to reflect on what we are offering, and to reflect on our attitudes with regard to giving. This is one aspect of making sure we are worthy recipients. It underscores the fact that our relationship with those who support us is one of mutual generosity, which is in itself, a great blessing.

Now just consider the culture of virtue that's been established here. We've all committed ourselves to living in a virtuous way, with integrity, according to the moral precepts. That too is a blessing, to live in a situation where there is this quality of integrity and trust. It supports, uplifts, and encourages us.

These are some of the many blessings that we're virtually swimming in here. By bringing them to mind, we are able to share and dedicate them. They can become a field of blessing and merit, not just for ourselves, but for others as well. Attending to our blessings, bringing them to mind, reflecting on this field of merit—this is important to do as we go through our day.

The foundation for this practice is selflessness. That's what really brings about the sense of merit and blessing—we are willing to set aside our personal agendas and preferences, our views and opinions, and everything that comes out of our obsession with "me" and "mine." Certainly, these things come to the surface in all of us, and I'm not suggesting we deny or try to annihilate them. Rather, this is about redirecting our attention away from self-oriented concerns so that we can step into this field of blessing and merit.

There is a verse from the Dhammapada where the Buddha instructs us to do things that are aligned with what is good and meritorious. He encourages us to do them over and over again because, as we develop an affinity for acting in that way, it will lead to our ease and well-being. This certainly applies to the practice of dedicating merit and blessings. It is something that can hold us in a place of ease; and if we are grounded in that place as we apply effort in our practice, our efforts will be held within that same quality of easefulness.

There is a lightness to experience when people live with a sense of generosity and selflessness. We can share in that, and dedicate the goodness of merit and blessings that come from it.

Gestures of Respect

Ajahn Yatiko • September 2012

Yesterday I clearly saw a defilement in myself that I'd like to speak about and share with you, so you can follow along with my process and possibly make use of it yourselves.

In the morning, I was putting out seats for *pūjā* on the ordination platform. For a long time I'd been resistant to the idea of putting out a seat for Luang Por Pasanno when he's away, as he is now. There seems to be an ambiguity about whether we put out a seat for him when he's gone. Sometimes we do, sometimes we don't. There's no established etiquette for this.

I had the thought, *He's not here, what's the point?* In the past, whenever someone put a seat out for him, something in my heart would roll its figurative eyes. But yesterday morning, as this reaction was coming up, I recognized what an unpleasant mind state it was. I said to myself, *Wait a minute. Putting out a seat is an act of respect for Luang Por. Luang Por is our teacher, who has given us so much and helped us in so many ways that we know and don't know. This act reminds us of his presence in the monastery as the leader of the community.* So when I did put out a seat for him, it came with a nice feeling of relief to know that I could overcome this defilement of which I was previously unaware.

It reminded me of Ajahn Sumedho's story about washing Ajahn Chah's feet. When Ajahn Chah would come back from alms round, twenty monks would come running out to wash his feet. Ajahn Sumedho would roll his eyes and think how stupid it

140

looked for twenty grown men to be washing one man's feet. He thought this was ridiculous and said to himself, *I'm never going to do that.* This happened day after day, until he eventually realized that having this thought was causing him suffering. The next day there were twenty-one monks washing Ajahn Chah's feet; Ajahn Sumedho enjoyed doing it and felt really good about it.

By bringing this up, I'm not saying that putting out a seat should now be established as monastery etiquette; I don't feel so strongly about it, and if someone does not set out a seat, I think that's okay. Rather, I'm trying to encourage us all to reflect on our attitudes about respect and to question why we feel the way we do. We can simply ask ourselves whether these attitudes are causing us to suffer in any way.

By examining our attitude in this way, we might find that we have a sense of relief when we choose an attitude that leads to a bright mind state instead of an unpleasant one. Showing respect is a nice thing; it brings up a nice feeling. It doesn't matter if people criticize us or think showing respect is stupid. If we do something that feels right, that feels kind, then it is a good thing to do. At the same time, it is not as if we are following a rule. It comes from free choice, and that's what makes it beautiful. If this were a rule and we put out a seat with a sense that this is what we were supposed to do, that wouldn't feel very special. It needs to come from the heart. When it does come from the heart there is an attitude we can have of wanting to use whatever opportunities are available to show respect and be reminded of something good, something uplifting.

We can use that attitude in our practice no matter what situation we find ourselves in. We can do something that is good or kind for another person. We can be forgiving, patient, thoughtful, and helpful with each other. This is the foundation of group harmony. We have a harmonious community of both laypeople and monastics, and that harmony has its foundation in mutual respect.

Rehearsing the Mood

Ajahn Jotipālo • December 2013

In communicating with other people there is always room for mistakes to be made and issues to come up around misunderstandings. When these problems occur, we can sometimes find it helpful to seek advice from someone else to help clarify what we want to say to the person we're having problems with. We do this so the next time we speak with that person, we will be speaking factually and at an appropriate time.

I was listening to a talk by Ajahn Soṇa and he gave a beautiful piece of advice in regards to this type of situation. Once we are clear about wishing to speak with someone in regards to a previous interaction, Ajahn Soṇa suggested, "Don't rehearse the story or what we want to say; instead, rehearse the mood, rehearse the state of mind we want to be in when we speak."

Do we want to be experiencing anger when we speak to the other person? If we really want to alienate ourselves and encourage that person to get upset, then we can rehearse anger. But if we want to help the other person or decrease tensions, then we can rehearse a compassionate mood or one based on loving-kindness. We can encourage that in ourselves.

This isn't only useful when we wish to speak with someone about an issue. We can do this all the time. We can contemplate and encourage the moods we wish to establish in our minds. While we are working with someone, for example, we can ask ourselves, *What's the mood I want to be in right now?* If we can deliberately generate a wholesome mood within ourselves, we allow our minds to more easily open to the Dhamma.

Sweep What's in Front of Your Broom

Luang Por Pasanno • August 2012

We have a very full schedule here at the monastery over the coming days. That's how it is, sometimes there's a lot happening. When this occurs, it's helpful to have a perspective that doesn't make things complicated or difficult.

I remember at Wat Nanachat, one of the things visitors were asked to do in the morning while the monks were out on alms round was to sweep the monastery grounds—and it's a fairly large monastery. One morning, while an *anagārika* was sweeping, a new guest came out, looked at the grounds, and said, "Are we supposed to sweep all of this?" The anagārika replied, "No, just what's in front of your broom." It's helpful to keep this sort of perspective.

But we can easily stray from that and tell ourselves, *Oh, there's this to do, and that to do; there's this person, and then that person.* It turns into something that sounds complicated and overwhelming. In the end, though, it's just the person in front of us that we're dealing with, the particular chore or task that needs to be done now, breathing in and breathing out, moment by moment.

Here in the monastery, once the morning work period is over and the meal is finished, then there's the afternoon. Take the time in the afternoon for meditation, for reading Dhamma, for some quiet time. No need to think about the things that may need doing in the future.

Remember that it's only what's in front of us that needs to be done. As we maintain that perspective, we realize that things do get done. They may not get done as quickly as we wish, or in the way we think they ought to be done, but we can only do what we're doing. It's helpful if we don't lose ourselves in a lot of thinking and complication.

That's a big part of personal practice. Without that we might start thinking of all of the things we need to do to become a proficient meditator or practitioner: *I've got to get my precepts down, learn the Vinaya, learn the chanting, get this meditation technique working and that other technique as well. There is this other technique I haven't even tried yet. There is this reflection I don't know and that aspect of Buddhist philosophy that I have to understand.* Then we might think, *Oh, this is hopeless. I'm just giving myself more suffering and more difficulty than I ever had before!*

But if we drop all of that and attend to just one breath at a time, to one mental state at a time, and that's all—if we can attend to things from that perspective—then everything is doable.

Clinging to Solidity

Ajahn Karuṇadhammo • November 2012

Last night Ajahn Amaro shared some reflections around the theme of transience and its relation to impermanence. After his talk I was contemplating this theme, especially around the sense of permanence and how we relate permanence to solidity. It is one of the fundamental delusions we carry around with us much of the time, and it forms the basis for a false sense of self, a solid "me" in this body. The quality of holding onto the perception of permanence is what leads to so much distress and suffering. It's good to get an understanding of how to bring that into conscious awareness as much as possible, not only in meditation, but when moving through the day.

When we maintain the sense of apparent permanence or solidity, it appears to be bound up with a fundamental motion of mind, the quality of clinging. In the suttas, the classic approach to having insight into this quality of clinging is by contemplating impermanence. This contemplation can give rise to a sense of dispassion, disenchantment, and can result in the ability to let go and release the clinging.

Alternatively, we can notice the sense of holding on to *any-thing* and use that as a basis for letting go of the perception of permanence and solidity. We then see how much difficulty it causes when we're involved with work or interaction with people, and there's this sense of holding on. I find it useful to go directly to the mind-motion of holding onto something and watch how it reinforces the sense of solidity, permanence, and a false reality. When we cling or hold tightly to some notion or opinion, as a result, everything becomes more concrete, more focused on the subject and object, more about "me"—more entangled and involved.

The views we cling to all tend to play with, feed on, and support each other. We can attack them from different angles, whether it's directly contemplating the transience of a particular situation or whether we can see the clinging or holding onto something. In that process of recognition, it's possible to realize, *I can drop this. I don't need to hold onto this. I can let it go.* We might then notice the sense of ease in the mind that comes when we are able to do that. We may also gain insight into the impermanence that appears right there, because if we don't hold onto something then it just moves on by itself. As quickly as it appears, it passes away, particularly in the realm of feelings, perceptions, and moods. When we don't hold onto those experiences, we see how quickly they change, morph, disappear, reappear, and disappear again.

The perception of transience makes the process of going through life much lighter; the burden doesn't have to be so heavy from holding on. So we can practice that throughout the day, taking moments to stop, seeing where there's holding and clinging, and then relaxing and letting go, allowing things to move on in their own natural way. Through this process we gain insight into the true nature of impermanence.

The Experience of Change

Luang Por Pasanno • June 2013

The weather these days is itself giving us something to reflect upon: Yesterday and last night it was raining. This weekend it's expected to be over 100 degrees. It should be obvious to us that this is definitely uncertain! Ajahn Chah kept encouraging us to investigate the truth of uncertainty—that the nature of things is "not sure"—and to resist the inner voice that says, *Without a doubt, things are going to be like this, or like that.*

Of course, the external environment is only one source of uncertainty; there's the internal environment, as well—our moods, perceptions, thoughts, and feelings—and it's this internal environment that's most important to examine. Sometimes we may think, *My practice is going well. My practice is moving in the right direction. It's really a sure thing ...* and then it changes. Other times we're feeling stuck in a pit of difficulties and may think, *This is really what I am, and everything is hopeless. This is a sure thing ...* and that too changes. It's important to point the mind toward the experience of change, uncertainty, and impermanence, so it can see the true nature of things. Doing this creates a sense of stability and develops the mind's capability to know things—to know when we're upset; to know when we're peaceful; to know when we're experiencing something wholesome. This quality of knowing is our place of refuge.

The uncertainty of things is simply how they are. But it's the way we *respond* to uncertainty that we need to focus on.

That's what reveals the areas in which we have more work to do, and the areas in which we have a good handle on the practice. What happens when we experience some difficulty and anger arises? What happens when we get what we want and an experience of happiness and well-being arises? How do we respond to that? Do we take it for granted? Do we make assumptions? Do we create certainty around it? Do we get caught up in it? Do we create a sense of self around it?

Working with uncertainty in this way is our practice. It's what gives us the opportunity to realize true peace. True peace cannot be found in a passing mood or a state of mind. True peace comes through recognizing the fundamentally uncertain nature of things.

As we go through our day, there's a constant, ongoing flow of change. Pay attention to that. Whether doing chores, engaging with people, sitting in formal meditation—be attentive, without forcing the mind in any way. This is how we can strengthen our place of refuge, the quality of clear knowing.

Listening to Reflections

Ajahn Yatiko • May 2013

I'd like to share an experience I've had, with the intention to say something useful—to plant some seeds. Sometimes when monastery residents or visitors attend these morning reflections, they can place the teacher on a pedestal, as if he is about to say something that will magically bring them insight, but after listening for a minute or so, they make up their minds that nothing worthwhile is being said and then tune out. It's as if they feel it's the teacher's responsibility to infuse them with something profound. But it's not. As listeners, it is *our* responsibility to pay attention and extract meaning from whatever is said. It's up to us. That's a change in attitude from simply expecting the teacher to have all the information and deliver something of value while we remain seated passively. With a different attitude we could say to ourselves, *I'm the one with the power here. It's my life, and I have to do what is going to be beneficial and meaningful for myself.*

We should remember that. When a teacher has finished offering a short reflection—whatever has been said—we're the ones who have to take responsibility for its impact. What are we going to do with what's been said? The teacher's reflection can be something extremely simple. But if we are listening to it with the right attitude and in the right way, it can trigger something very valuable in our minds and hearts. Conversely, we might hear a talk that is extremely profound, rich, deep,

151

subtle, and meaningful. However, if we are only sitting here because we always sit here at this time of day or we do not make an effort to extract meaning from what is said, then we are not going to get anything out of it. It all comes down to the quality of attention we bring to the present moment and how we listen to the Dhamma.

Breathing Into Busy Activity

Luang Por Pasanno • June 2005

There has been a lot of busyness here these days. Many things need to be done, and we're doing them. But it's important to be careful about how much we get swept up into the busyness of our lives. Those are two different things—the doing of a task and the frantic, busy, scattered energy we may bring to the task. We can try to watch and reflect on the feeling behind what we're doing. What is the energy behind it? Recognize where the feeling of agitation comes from.

Much depends upon staying with the breathing—breathing into the activity of what we're doing. Sometimes it helps to step back, relax, and slow down. That doesn't mean we accomplish less. Oftentimes, the more frantic we become, the less we accomplish. In addition, being frantic obstructs the enjoyment of what we're doing and may compromise our harmony with others. So pay attention to breathing and relaxing.

We also need to be careful not to take on too many things at once. However, it's more the attitude we carry in our mind that's the problem, because we can really only do one thing at a time. We carry around in our minds all the things we think we have to do, and that stirs up this frantic energy.

We deal with this by breathing into what we are doing, being with it, and not getting too swept up. Make the breath a force for settling. It can be very satisfying paying attention to the breath, the body, and the actions involved in the task we're doing. The more we attend to the body while we are engaged, the more we can generate a sense of focus and well-being in the midst of activity.

Right Action Guided by Internal Experience

Ajahn Amaro • December 2008

Sammā kammanta—right action—is an essential factor of the Noble Eightfold Path. Often the Eightfold Path is summarized as *sīla*, *samādhi*, and *paññā*, virtue, concentration, and wisdom. Right action is then woven into the section on sīla, along with right speech and right livelihood. As a result, when we are considering meditation, we may focus on the samādhi section of the path and forget the influence right action has on our minds and states of consciousness throughout the day, as well as when we meditate.

Often during the course of our lives in the monastery, because we have a prescribed set of rules for conduct and a prescribed routine, we can miss the effects that actions have on our minds, our states of consciousness. It's something to be alert to. What we do and say during the day have an effect, and that effect leads to either our spiritual growth or our degeneration. Because action has such an effect, the monastery environment is designed to maximize the wholesome qualities and to restrain the unwholesome qualities.

But even within the framework of the precepts we live by and the routine we have, it's good to be alert, recognizing the effect on the mind of the actions we perform and the things we say during the course of the day. It's good to consciously notice—when we've acted or spoken in an unskillful way—how much that sticks in the mind. When we're sitting down to meditate, we can see the difference. At the end of the day, when there has been a very good standard of restraint and clarity, then during the evening sitting we may notice, *Oh, look, there's nothing on my mind. I'm not remembering anything cruel or selfish or coarse that I said today. I'm not feeling the effects of having been agitated or uncontrolled in my actions. Look at that, there's an absence of unpleasant results.* We don't always notice that, but it is quite helpful to our practice if we do.

It's easier to notice, at the end of the day, those times when we've had some kind of contentious exchange or have used our speech in an uncontrolled or obstructive way. On days like those, that's often what's on the mind during the evening sitting. We sit down and suddenly—*boom*—there it is, that regrettable conversation is replaying itself. These unfortunate episodes arise immediately in the mind and then, quite often, they can occupy the entire sitting. They can keep popping up over and over again.

It's not necessary to create a sense of guilt, self-hatred or self-criticism. But it is helpful when we think, *Oh, look—this was the action, that is the result. Because this was done, there is that effect. This is the cause, and that is the result.* That clear observation of the causality of our experience is the doorway to wisdom, concentration, and clarity. The more clearly we see the effects in meditation of unskillful actions, the more clearly we realize we are simply putting obstacles in our own way and sabotaging our own efforts. Then we ask ourselves, *Why would I want to do this? Why on earth do I want to mess up my own living space like this?* It's as if we're grabbing handfuls of rocks and earth and fistfuls of poison oak and sprinkling them all around the inside of our *kuṭis. Why would I want to do that? What a strange, stupid thing to do.* This becomes clear to us.

When we reflect on wholesome and unwholesome mind states and recognize their effects on how we act and speak, then that very recognition of cause-and-effect guides us. It helps support our efforts to be more restrained in the future. It's not because there's a set of external rules telling us that we should be like this, or because we fear an authority figure who's going to scold us if we do something wrong. We simply see for ourselves that right action supports the cultivation of a pleasant, wholesome abiding, and it allows us to fulfill the purpose for which we came to live at the monastery. Through right action we are setting the conditions in favor of our purpose, steering our life in a way that supports it. We're simply doing ourselves a favor, which brings blessings into our lives.

It's not that we're never going to make mistakes or lose our way. But we can cultivate that sense of attention and, by seeing how action and speech affect the mind, we can let that recognition inform the way we operate and speak. Then later, when we find ourselves being drawn into an unskillful conversation or getting self-centered, aggressive, or lazy, we can let that experience of recognizing cause-and-effect guide us. *The last time I did that, it took me three days to get over it. It seemed like a good idea at the time, but there was a lot of wreckage left behind after acting in that way.* Because of having seen for ourselves the painful effects of unskillful actions, we find ourselves respecting and moving toward restraint, modesty, simplicity, and inner quietude. This is really the best kind of training. Training in terms of being obedient to an external force has its place. But being obedient to and guided by our own internal experience—that's the kind of training that brings well-grounded, long-lasting results.

According With Conditions

Luang Por Pasanno • June 2013

In terms of living as monastics and lay practitioners, there are two helpful principles we can return to again and again in our daily life. The first of these is learning how to accept and adapt to whatever conditions we find ourselves in. This doesn't mean being indifferent or not dealing with things, but really engaging with conditions in a skillful, attentive way. With so many visitors coming to the monastery today we may think, *I don't want this; it's not how I like it.* Or we may welcome the interaction and find ourselves drawn into that contact. Neither reaction is very skillful. The wholesome alternative is to be mindful of the ways we react to the various conditions we encounter. What are our habits? How can we develop habits that better accord with Dhamma, that accord with changing conditions so that a sense of equanimity and balance is more readily available to us? That's very much a part of monastic training in this lineage—and how Ajahn Chah trained the monks who came to live with him.

The second principle is renunciation—*nekkhamma*—which is an integral part of adapting to conditions. The English word *renunciation* suggests that we're pushing away or running away from something. But that doesn't reflect the real meaning of nekkhamma, which is a sense of rising up to conditions with a noble attitude. It's a quality that brightens the mind and allows us to engage with the Dhamma. If we neglect opportunities to practice nekkhamma, we miss much of what monastery training is for. Ajahn Chah used to speak about people who became discontented while practicing in a monastery. They might leave and go out into the forest, which was fine for a while, but then they'd get fed up with the forest and go off to the seashore to practice, and after a while they'd get fed up with that, so they would go off to the mountains, and after a while they'd get fed up with that too. They neglected to practice renunciation in the circumstances they were in—they didn't engage or rise up to that opportunity.

So in our daily lives, it's important that we apply these two training principles: accepting and adapting to conditions, while sustaining a noble attitude of renunciation. These principles can serve as aspirations for everybody, lay and monastic, because we're all apt to spend so much time and effort trying to manipulate circumstances to get what we want, grumbling and complaining about how things are. Instead, we can learn to accommodate, rise up, and meet conditions with a sense of relinquishment, letting go of discontent. When we practice like this we are likely to find that there is no need to make conditions into a problem for ourselves.

What Does It Mean to Listen?

Ajahn Yatiko • November 2012

What does it mean to listen? How many difficulties arise simply through poor listening skills and not allowing others the space to say what they want to say? It's not easy to find people who know how to simply listen. A good listener doesn't focus on the content of what is being said. Whether it's good or bad is not the point. The point is to simply listen, to let people be what they are. This holds true for listening to oneself, as well.

There's the mind state of listening and the mind state of judging, and they are completely different experiences. There is an open, spacious, attentive, and awake quality inherent in a mind that is truly listening. Suppose everybody in this room right now had what we might call a listening mind state, a state in which the mind is sensitive and open. Given this shared quality, if everyone were to move around in the room, coming in and out of everybody else's personal space, there would probably be a sense of harmony. Compare that to a room filled with twenty or thirty people holding tightly to some judgment or view. It's likely that if they were all to move about the room, it would be clank-and-clunk, everybody stumbling into each other's space in some sort of disharmonious way. So listening, and its quality of attentive spaciousness, is a beautiful skill to develop.

Truly listening allows things to be the way they are. It allows us to be what we are. I'm not saying we should ignore those aspects of our lives and our practice that clearly need work and attending to. But I think most of us are already pretty good at thinking of the 101 ways we could be better. What we often neglect, however, is the wish to be heard, which is a wish that everyone has. Responding to that wish with compassion requires that we develop the skill of receptive, non-judgmental listening—listening to others and listening to ourselves.

Death at a Distance

Ajahn Karuṇadhammo • October 2013

The contemplations of old age, sickness, and death are themes that seem to be repeating themselves these days. Iris's recent diagnosis of lung cancer is just one example. Based on my own experience of having been a nurse, it is interesting to see how the mind immediately moves toward the technical aspects of the illness: *What kind of tumor is it? What is the staging? What are the treatment options? What are the services that are available?* This is all based on my conditioning and background. Then sometimes I move into: *How is this for Iris? What is she going through? What kind of resources does it take to deal with this kind of information? How is she coping with this? What can I do to help her? How can I be most attentive without being overly solicitous?*

I recognize, both in myself and others, that this kind of speculation and questioning are expressions of a truly noble concern for what Iris's experience may be like and how we want to help. In some ways, though, as we try to help we can take the focus off our own experiences and put off the need to reflect on ourselves. Many of the Buddha's teachings encourage us to pay attention to and contemplate the body in terms of aging, sickness, and death, especially as these subjects relate to ourselves. Nonetheless, it is difficult to acknowledge this until we find ourselves experiencing this on a personal level. So we continue to think about that other person and her problem, hoping that by externalizing it in those noble ways, we might somehow be able keep old age, sickness, and death at a distance.

How can we internalize these thoughts? How can we remind ourselves that old age, sickness, and death is about me? We can say things to ourselves like, *This will happen to me sometime in the future.* But that is another great way of putting a bit of a distance between ourselves and reality. What we need to do is adjust our views so we can see that not only is this happening out there to other people, or have some vague notion of it occurring in the future for ourselves, but right now, *This is my body that is aging, and there might actually be something happening to me now, in the present.* Then what does that mean? How should we contemplate that? This body is incredibly sensitive and fragile. We can be sensitive to the feelings of the body, the sensations, and come to understand the body as a sensitive and fragile condition of elements brought together by natural factors. It's an exceptionally delicate balance which can be lost at any moment. Just as Iris has a tumor in her lungs and tumors throughout her body, we can imagine that happening in our own bodies and take it to heart.

Try to do that as a daily reflection. If we are frequently able to bring this perception to mind, then the more real it will become for us. Paradoxically, this reflection can bring up a sense of ease and calm. This settled quality arises from insight into the characteristics of *anicca* and *anattā*, impermanence and not-self. Both characteristics become more apparent and real, so that when serious illness or imminent death approaches there will be a familiarity with the nature of one's finite existence. The more those familiar feelings can be brought in, the less fear there is around letting go of that which really isn't ours to hold onto in the first place.

Earthworm Practice

Luang Por Pasanno • November 2008

With the drawbacks of physical existence, the Buddha instructed that we reflect on the theme of death as an antidote to our interest in being reborn into the conditioned realm. These reflections are meant to bring up a sense of urgency: There is no time to waste. There aren't unlimited opportunities for spiritual practice. We have excellent conditions right now, and we should make use of them. The image that the Buddha uses for this sense of urgency is a person whose hair is on fire. There's a real motivation to put that out, to deal with the situation.

It's easy to put things off, to find various good and logical excuses to be pulling back a bit on our effort. The motivation for making the effort, for putting attention back onto the practice, can lose its quality of urgency. We may turn to some social engagement, some conversation, some distraction, and it might be interesting, it might have some tangential benefit, but we must realize the need to set that aside and return to being mindfully attentive to what we're doing.

One of the problems with having a sense of urgency is the feeling of flailing around—putting out effort in a sporadic way and not being able to sustain it. We start off enthusiastically, really buckling down, *Okay, back to the practice, I'm really going to stick with it this time.* Yet we're not able to sustain it. We swing back and forth. Sometimes the results of our efforts might not seem so dazzling. They might not make us think, *Now I'm really getting somewhere!* They may not even seem interesting. So we can get frustrated and pull back and then, sometime later, it's *Okay, time to buckle down again.* But consistency is what's important and paying attention to being consistent.

I remember Ajahn Chah's advice on how to maintain constancy in the practice, addressing the issue of first wanting to really push and then feeling frustrated, "Can you learn to practice like an earthworm? They can't know where they're going, but they keep moving along. So get your head down, simply go forward, just have earthworm practice. Keep moving, constant and consistent."

If It Doesn't Die, Make It Good

Ajahn Ñāṇiko • November 2013

It's important to reflect on the habits we have, to ask ourselves, *Does this habit help to make the mind more peaceful, or does it tend to make the mind more agitated?* The Thai Forest ajahns often use the phrase *plien nisai*, which means "to change habits." In the Thai Forest Tradition there is a strong emphasis on changing one's unskillful habits. Our chanting includes the "Ten Subjects for Frequent Recollection by Monastics," where we recite, "I will strive to abandon my former habits. This should be reflected upon again and again by one who has gone forth" (AN 10.48).

Habits run deep, and they're very difficult to change. But if we have a habit and notice that it's causing us to be agitated, or if we are habitually irritated by something, we can use the Buddha's teachings any time of the day to change our direction.

I remember Ajahn Jayasāro telling a group of us in Thailand, "If you are keeping *sīla*, then no matter what lifestyle you are leading—even if you are not meditating much—all day is an opportunity to be letting go of defilement and training the mind." So whether we are working, meditating, or whatever, there's always an opening for us to change our obstructive habits. It takes mindfulness to see our habits, and it takes effort and patience to change those habits, but it is possible—and vital—to do.

As Ajahn Chah said: "If it isn't good, let it die. If it doesn't die, make it good." Sometimes we have a habit we can't let go of. We try to let it die, we don't feed it, but it's so strong that we can't let go. In cases like that, we need to "make it good." We need to steer it in a different direction. As we go about our day we can attend to our habits and little by little steer these habits in the direction of the skillful and wholesome.

A Bowl Full of Light

Luang Por Pasanno • August 2013

I have been reading a book on Hawaiian spirituality and there's a beautiful image that Hawaiians use. Each one of us is born into the world with a bowl full of light and for each unskillful choice we make throughout our lives—getting caught up in anger, conflict, or selfishness—it's as if we put a rock in the bowl. The more rocks that are placed in the bowl, the less room there is for light.

In our daily life practice, by examining what it is we are doing, we can reflect on whether we are a being of light or a being of rocks and pebbles. When we recognize that we have accumulated any kind of rocks or pebbles, we learn how to tip over the bowl and dump the rocks out. This helps us look after that bowl of light and return to making choices that are more skillful.

Light is a universal image that is used across all religious and spiritual traditions. In the first discourse of the Buddha, the Dhammacakkappavattana Sutta, there is the contemplation of the Four Noble Truths and the implementing of the Eightfold Path. The stock phrases that follow this are: *cakkhuṃ udapādi, ñāṇaṃ udapādi, paññā udapādi, vijjā udapādi, āloko udapādi*—vision arises, knowledge arises, wisdom arises, clear seeing arises, and light arises. There is a sense of light coming into being. From the Buddhist perspective, when we establish and develop a continuity of training with the Four Noble

Truths and the Eightfold Path, it brings light into the mind and into our being.

Looking Back on the Effort

Ajahn Yatiko • July 2012

Yesterday, Luang Por Sopah was giving some reflections about Wat Pa Pong and what it was like in the early days. While Luang Por spoke, I looked over at Ajahn Pasanno and saw him smiling brightly as he listened. I could almost see the wheels in Ajahn Pasanno's head turning as his memories were being churned up. It seemed to me that he might have been thinking, *I know what Luang Por Sopah is talking about, and no one else here can really know what it was like living with Luang Por Chah. But I do know and I do remember.*

I recall somebody saying once that after years of difficult practice have passed and time has put some perspective on one's life, then one can look back on all the effort and suffering involved in the practice with real appreciation, delight, and gratitude. This is very different from the suffering that arises when one becomes obsessed with personal ambitions, worries, and concerns. When we look back on those sorts of past experiences, there tends to be a feeling of loss and a sense of time wasted.

But again, when we look back at the effort we have put into our practice, how we have endured and cultivated the path, the beautiful teachings that we loved, respected, imbibed, and listened to, then the heart feels bright, warm, soft, and rich. That's something that I thought I clearly saw in Ajahn Pasanno yesterday as Luang Por Sopah was recollecting his life at Wat Pa Pong.

We can lose touch with the inspiring memories of our wholesome efforts due to the immediacy of the daily difficulties, frustrations, and temporary setbacks we experience. With these daily concerns, we can easily forget that we're engaged in something very beautiful and noble. So from time to time, we need uplifting, we need to refresh ourselves, and that's where these inspiring memories of our past efforts come in. They can uplift and refresh our practice and are worth bringing up, reflecting upon, and appreciating. They remind us that we have been engaged in something very beautiful and noble, indeed.

It's Not a Sure Thing

Luang Por Pasanno • June 2012

It is the commemoration of Ajahn Chah's birthday today. One of the constant refrains in his teaching and training is the recollection of the Thai phrase, *mynair*—unsure, uncertain, not a sure thing. We can develop the ability to hold experience in this space of not sure and uncertainty. Often the mind inclines to some sort of story, *It's going to be just like this; this is going to be really wonderful; that is going to be great.* But the challenge is remembering that it's just a story, it's not a sure thing. The mind can also buy into, *It's going to be awful; it's going to be dreadful; how am I going to bear with this?* What can help us with this is thinking, *it's not a sure thing.* We develop the ability to hold experience within the framework of mindfulness, reflection, investigation, and discernment, and openly acknowledge that we're not sure what it's going to be like. When we hold experience in this way, we find that everything is bearable, everything is quite all right—we are creating a framework of Dhamma rather than a framework of our own reactions and habits.

Straightforward and Gentle in Speech

Ajahn Karuṇadhammo • April 2013

Many of our teachers, especially in the West, speak about the need to adapt to modern circumstances while continuing to adhere to principles. One of these principles is concerned with wholesome and unwholesome courses of action—right speech. I was thinking about the need for us to adapt to different circumstances and cultures when we interact and converse. An example of this might be seen in the communication differences between monastics in a new Western monastery and in a monastery in Thailand. We have a high level of engagement here at Abhayagiri, partially due to the nature of building a monastery and trying to form a community. There tends to be more interaction and speech during work periods and sometimes this requires quick communication while we are attending to our chores. With this type of communication there is a necessity for being mindful with our speech. We need to be careful how we apply the guidelines of right speech and interact with each other in thoughtful and caring ways.

A line that comes to mind is in the Mettā Sutta, "straightforward and gentle in speech" (Sn 1.8)—it's a combination of two different actions. We aren't just straightforward, but also gentle, nor are we merely gentle; we need to be straightforward. It's both qualities at the same time. This is often not an easy task—it takes a tremendous amount of skill and mindfulness to be straightforward and gentle simultaneously. It's easy to become straightforward when there is something we think is wrong, something we think should be done in a particular way, when we're in a rush to finish, or a previous interaction has led to some negativity. We can easily be straightforward in those circumstances and not consider the more gentle approach. During those times we can blurt something out that is a bit too aggressive, demanding, harsh, or simply not considerate. When we are speaking, it's important to monitor our energy so that we are communicating what needs to be communicated in a straightforward, clear manner while also remaining aware of the energetic impact of such speech—how what we say might affect the people around us. We can consider the impact a gentle quality has on communication, thinking, *How would I like this message delivered to me if I were on the receiving end?*

Conversely, people can be overly concerned about how something is communicated because they do not want to upset anyone, cause any discord, or are afraid of someone's reaction. When this occurs, the message may be delivered in a way that is indirect, uncertain, or not straightforward at all, and therefore, the content of what is being said and its meaning is misunderstood. Perhaps one is communicating out of fear—afraid to speak up in a situation where someone needs a clear statement. We can end up being imprecise or ambiguous, thinking that we've communicated a message, but the other person has not heard a word of what needed to be said.

Being able to combine clarity, honesty, gentleness, and kindness in what we say is a skill that requires a lot of attention and work. We are learning to consider both how our speech is delivered and how it will be received. I find for myself that it's an ongoing exercise of making mistakes and learning, going back and apologizing, and if necessary, re-clarifying what it was I was trying to say in the first place. It's a meaningful and significant part of the practice and something that I believe is at the core of our daily lives.

The Development of Equanimity

Ajahn Amaro • November 2008

When we do the chanting on the four divine abodes, the *brahmavihāras*—*mettā, karuṇā, muditā, upekkhā*, loving-kindness, compassion, appreciative joy, equanimity—going through each one, it's important to notice the development of equanimity around reflections on kamma, actions of cause and effect. "I am the owner of my kamma, heir to my kamma, born of my kamma, related to my kamma, abide supported by my kamma. Whatever kamma I shall do, for good or for ill, of that I will be the heir."

The other brahmavihāras—mettā, karuṇā, and muditā—have an emotional tone, a quality of wishing well to ourselves and others, of wishing to be free from suffering. But the fourth one, upekkhā, equanimity, is developed through a conscious reflection on kamma and *vipāka kamma*, action and its results. That may not sound terribly interesting, and so it can easily be pushed aside. But equanimity is the most refined of the brahmavihāras. It's quite a significant mental quality and is difficult to establish.

When we consciously reflect on cause and effect, we can distinguish one from the other in our direct experience, *Ah, this is the cause of that result.* Or with greater detail, *Because I've been generous and kind and I've been keeping the precepts well, then an inner lightness and confidence in my own goodness has developed.* Or *Because I've been selfish, deceitful, clumsy, casual, or sloppy, there's this feeling of regret, self-criticism, and a negative emotional tone.* This is a very conscious way of letting go of the content of happiness or unhappiness and seeing clearly for ourselves, *Because of this good action, there's a pleasant result. Because of this unskillful action, there's an unpleasant result. I see.* It's the law of nature—because of this, there is that. It's the Dhamma in action. It's extraordinarily simple, and when we see it clearly, it takes a huge amount of the alienation and burden away from our experiences. This is not a small thing—it's essential to our practice.

As soon as the mind sees things in terms of right and wrong, when it buys into those kinds of judgments, equanimity is lost. *This is right. This is the right way to do it. That's wrong. That's the wrong way to do it. He shouldn't be doing it that way. He should be doing it this way.* But by cultivating equanimity, we can reflect and see more clearly, *I'm calling that "right" because of what? Because of the conventions of Theravada Buddhism? Or, I'm calling this "right" because of my understanding of the mechanics of the hillside? Or how the drainage channels work?* We can more clearly see how our conditioning leaps onto those judgments, saying, *This is absolutely right, that is absolutely wrong. It should be this way. It shouldn't be that way.* We believe it over and over again, a thousand times a day. We believe in our judgments and take them to be absolutely real. But with some equanimity, the mind has the ability to recognize that this is called "right" because of a reason, and this is called "wrong" because of a reason. There's a cause, and "right" and "wrong" are simply effects.

Consider reflecting on a simple thing like eating. Because we have human bodies, we become hungry and need to eat. Needing to keep the body going to sustain life is the cause, needing to eat is the effect. When we eat we choose what to use to keep the body going. This effect appears as likes and dislikes, rights and wrongs. The mind chatters away, *That's great food. That's terrible food. He's really brilliant at cooking this. Oh no, he's ruined that again.* It's only because we need to eat food that those judgments arise. It's because of having a human body—needing to put stuff into these holes in our faces, chomp it up and swallow it down to sustain life—that we have any relationship at all to these plants and animals in this way. If we didn't have human bodies, if we were all in the *arūpa* realm where they have no bodies, then we wouldn't relate to fruit, vegetables, or meat in this way. None of that would be perceived as food—there wouldn't even be a word for physical food. It simply wouldn't concern us.

So this is an encouragement for all of us—particularly with the rainy weather, working outside in the rain, trickles of chilly water running down our necks and into our socks—to notice when the mind says *like* or *dislike*, *right* or *wrong*. Because it's the rainy season, these feelings might arise. This is the cause, and this is the effect. See how that small reflection can take us a step back from the notion that right, wrong, like, and dislike are objective or lasting realities. With that stepping back and seeing things more clearly, what we draw closer to is the brahmavihāra of equanimity.

An Internal Space of Mindfulness

Luang Por Pasanno • July 2012

Currently, there are many visiting monastics and laypeople here, and the numbers are at the high end of what we are used to. In some areas of the monastery there is limited space and close quarters. In the monk's room, the kitchen, and various other places where we are doing activities together we need to attend to the ways we interact with each other. It is easy to slip into frivolous, sarcastic, or negative speech that doesn't help us or anyone around us. When in proximity with people, try to maintain a mindful and respectful space. If we're not attentive to that, and barge into crowded places being pushy or anxious, it tends to have an agitating influence and is not particularly pleasant for anyone. So let's try to return to an inner space of mindfulness.

How do we maintain mindfulness? All of us living at the monastery are here because we are interested and inspired by the concepts of mindfulness and wisdom. But sometimes when we find ourselves in situations where we are more socially active and engaged than usual, mindfulness and wisdom fall by the wayside, and the result is not beautiful. Instead, we can pay special attention to maintaining mindfulness.

It's not that difficult to be mindful when we are on our own in our *kuṭis*. But when we're engaging with others, when there are duties that need to be done, or when something needs doing right away, it takes effort to stop ourselves from being swept up in agitation, and effort to maintain a space of mindfulness and letting go. What we are letting go of is suffering. When we use mindfulness and relinquishment, there's less suffering. With less mindfulness and less relinquishment, there is more suffering. It's a very simple equation, but one we can easily forget.

Following Rules: What's the Point?

Ajahn Yatiko • October 2012

Yesterday, in Vinaya class, we were talking about how we relate to rules. As monastics, we have so many rules that are a part of our lifestyle. There are countless rules that define the way we live and the way we do things. It's interesting to see how Western monks like us often relate to the rules in a fearful way. There's a sense of all these different rules in place, and we're trying to control and force ourselves to live within these different constraints. It can be daunting.

We've heard from various teachers that following rules is not an end in itself. Ajahn Sumedho speaks about Ajahn Chah as being a monk who was very scrupulous with the Vinaya rules, but who didn't look or act like a limited person. Certainly when I listen to Ajahn Chah's Dhamma teachings, they have a vitality that's incredibly fresh and vibrant. This seems related to how he followed the monastic discipline and rules while not being attached to those rules. For ourselves, however, we need to be careful and discerning in this particular area of non-attachment.

We often hear the phrase, "Don't get attached to rules." I remember when I first came across Buddhism, I found teachers who weren't "attached to rules" and sometimes ended up making a real mess out of their lives. It seemed their disciples suffered in many ways as well, because of this confused relationship with following a moral discipline. As a result of witnessing that, whenever I hear the phrase, "Don't be attached to rules," a red flag goes up for me, as well as a bit of fear. It's important to recognize the potential for self-deception or self-delusion when we take on this attitude and say to ourselves, *I'm not going to be attached to the rules.* We want to be cautious about this kind of attitude, because it can easily slip into following or not following some moral guideline simply based on our likes or dislikes. We can then throw out the rules we don't like anytime we feel they're getting in the way of satisfying a particular craving we have or avoiding some aversion. We go ahead and do as we please, regardless of the consequences it may have for us or others, based on the excuse, *I'm not attached to these rules.*

At the same time, it's important to remember that we're here to be free from suffering. Although these guidelines help us, we're not here to live by a bunch of rules that are going to force us into conforming, keeping us nice and safe, or making us so bland that we don't have any problems. That's not the Buddha's path to freedom. The Buddha's path is to find contentment within limitations. We have limitations, forms, and practices that serve as containers: the rules and standards of the Vinaya. These aren't conventions that we have to feel limited or constrained by. We can learn to relax around them, finding a sense of inner contentment as we follow them and keep them in mind.

We can start by approaching the present moment with a mind-set of self-acceptance, freedom, and contentment—a paradigm with which we don't have to be defined by rules or anything else. From that mind-set, we can see that all these rules we're living by are simply conventions. They don't have any ultimate reality that has to define us. If we can see that, contemplate that, and have a sense of expansiveness and open-ness around these conventions, then perhaps we can experience contentment within limitation. We can be free of the sense of constraint while living within constraint. We don't have to be held down by these rules and structures, because a feeling of real freedom is present within us. In that freedom, quite spontaneously, we might think, *It's not a problem to keep to these rules. This is quite all right. I'm very happy eating one meal a day. I don't mind wearing these robes like everyone else here, and being celibate is beneficial for my practice and my mind.*

This mind-set is quite different from feeling that we need to tightly control our behavior and constantly look around to see if anyone has spotted us making a mistake. When we have that sort of attitude, it can feel like there's no room to breathe. We might be able to live like this for a while, but I'm not convinced it's sustainable. It's a balancing act, and it can be quite tricky. We need to learn how to reflect on all this in a skillful way, recognizing the capacity for self-deception in the area of non-attachment to rules. Then again, we need to recognize that we haven't taken up the monastic life merely to perfect a litany of codes and standards. It's not about standards. That's not the point. It's about learning to find contentment within the context of conventions.

There may be a danger that what I've said this morning will be misunderstood. Do not think I'm suggesting that the rules should be tossed out or not respected. I'm simply offering these reflections for contemplation. How can we loosen our tight grip on the rules, while at the same time continuing to follow them, understanding that they are an essential part of the monastic path? Contemplating in this way takes intelligence and ingenuity, plus circumspection, to ensure that our reflections bring positive results that enrich and enliven our practice.

The Natural Result

Luang Por Pasanno • July 2012

This morning we chanted the Dhammacakkappavattana Sutta in English. There's always something that strikes me in that sutta, both hearing it and reflecting on it. For instance, the Buddha says the Middle Way and the Eightfold Path give knowledge and understanding and lead to peace and awakening. That's the function of the path. When we are aligned with the Middle Way, we are in balance—this happens naturally.

In Pāli the word *karaṇī*, as in *cakkhukaraṇī, ñāṇakaraṇī*, means "to make" or "to produce." It's an emphatic verb. This suggests that when we put our practice into balance, a good result will be produced. It's helpful to develop a sense of confidence in this natural cause-and-effect relationship.

How do we achieve this balance? Again, we align ourselves with the Middle Way, which means not getting caught by the extremes of either sensual indulgence or ascetic deprivation. We are not seeking delight, always looking for something to gratify ourselves, nor are we pushing things away, trying to get rid of them.

Ajahn Chah used to say that there are basically two desires in the mind: one is the desire to get something, which has the energy of moving toward; the other is the desire to get rid of something, not wanting to deal with it, which has the energy of pushing away. We see these two desires at work all the time—as we perform our tasks and duties, while engaging with people, and when we're off on our own. The mind tends to lean toward these two desires. It's not in balance; it's not following the Middle Way. But when we come back to a place of being attentive to balance, attentive to the Middle Way, bringing forth the factors of the path, then the natural results are knowledge and understanding and a sense of peace.

As we go about our daily chores, our day-to-day living in the monastery, we can make this simple effort of looking after the path, looking after those aspects of training the Buddha laid down for us. When we do this, we will produce the natural results of the Middle Way.

You're a Warrior Aren't You?

Ajahn Karuṇadhammo • May 2013

Last night we had a discussion about the power of practicing in community. One of the things I remember fondly about an experience in community was during my third Rains Retreat away at Chithurst Monastery in England. When I first arrived, I was trying to get my bearings and slowly familiarizing myself with some of the community members. One of the monks, who was just junior to me, sat on my left and I noticed after a number of weeks he wasn't engaging or making any contact. He was very quiet and reserved. I didn't know what to make of it. It was several weeks later that I began to think, *Well, perhaps he just doesn't like me or maybe I said something in the beginning that disturbed him.* At one point only he and I were in the day room resting after the meal. He had yet to say anything to me the entire time since I had arrived. I was sitting on one side of the room and he was sitting on the other and he broke into conversation, saying, "You're a warrior."

I thought, *What? What does he mean?* so I said to him, "What?"

He replied, "You're a warrior, aren't you?"

I thought to myself, *Well, I've never thought of myself as a warrior.* So I asked him: "What do you mean? Why do you say that I'm a warrior?"

He replied back to me, "Well, I know, because I'm a warrior, too."

I thought, *What's going on in this guy's mind?* Again I said, "What do you mean?"

He responded, "Well, I can see that you warry a lot. And I know that because I warry a lot too."

I thought, *Okay, now this makes sense*—I'd forgotten for a moment that I was in England and things like "worry" are pronounced a bit differently. This monk went on to explain that he had been suspicious of me for the first few weeks because I was an American, and he had many different preconceptions of what Americans were like and did not want to get too close or engage. As it turned out, we became good friends over the year and appreciated each other's company.

Last night here at the monastery, we were talking about living in community—the effect people have on us and how, particularly as Westerners, we have a strong individual self-identity and therefore construct so much *dukkha* around that identity. With this individualism in our culture, we don't have a lot of experience living in community, nor do we understand the benefits of living with and learning from other people in this way. Ajahn Chah's training heavily emphasized the power of living in community. It can be difficult to live this way because we all come from diverse backgrounds and have our different habits and ways of being in the world. But this kind of interaction, living and working with other people twenty-four hours a day, is a powerful practice.

I also briefly stayed at Amaravati during that same year. In the Amaravati kitchen, there was a vegetable-peeling machine that consisted of a big drum with a rough surface on the inside where vegetables whirled around. Carrots or potatoes were thrown into this machine, and they banged up against each other and against the rough surface of the drum until all the skins were peeled off. When I first saw this I thought, *Wow, this is just what living in community is like.* Part of it is the process of constantly being in a close living environment with other people until, over time, all the rough edges are worn down through interaction and give and take. There aren't a lot of people who would willingly throw themselves into a situation like a vegetable peeler, but that's basically what we have done here in the monastery.

There's a strength and power that we build up from engaging in formal meditation practice, being on our own, and establishing a sense of solitude. This is, of course, important in the Forest Tradition. But it's good to ask ourselves, *How much self-concern and self-identity can be let go of, worked with, and honed down through the practice of being in community?* As individuals, we really aren't as important as we think we are. All the mistakes we make, the expectations we have of ourselves and other people, the difficulties, criticisms of others, criticisms of ourselves—all of these rough edges need to be acknowledged and seen for what they are. This acknowledgment and understanding can't take place if we don't have that kind of bump and grind with other people to help expose those rough edges. It's not easy—none of the practice is that easy—but we learn to whittle away the rough edges through the use of community and through self-reflection about how we are engaging in community. We do this by letting go of the expectations for ourselves or other people to be a particular way. It's a powerful practice to establish a state of mind that is not so self-involved. When we talk about the practice of letting go of the ego, the self-identity, I think we need to reflect on the importance of communal life and how lucky we are to have it. While we are living with others we can depend on that structure of support and make full use of it.

Mindfully Waiting in the Present Moment

Ajahn Yatiko • June 2013

Sitting here in silence, some might say, feels like a waste of time. Sitting here waiting ... waiting for something to be said. It could be a waste of time if we are sitting here waiting mindlessly. But it is not a waste of time if there is mindfulness present and an awareness of the present moment.

Usually, at this time of day, there is a sense of anticipation as the work period draws near. There are thoughts about what we are going to do and what we don't want to do, all of which are influenced by the different attitudes that we have toward work. So this silence beforehand can sometimes bring up feelings of anxiety, and we might think, *Say something, it doesn't matter what it is, just say anything to fill the space.* Or the mind can slip into an animal state during which we zone out with eyes open, not really looking at anything. We are here, but not present. Our behavior is almost cow-like.

During this silence many different feelings and thoughts can arise, and we usually identify with them. We are like a fish caught with a hook and line that is simply pulling us along. But if mindfulness is present, we can see the hook and say to ourselves, *I don't trust that.* We have the mindfulness to recognize the presence of experience, the presence of feeling and thought, and we can think, *Wait a minute. This compulsion to*

attach and identify with the content of my consciousness is just like
the bait on the end of that hook; it's trying to get me to bite, and once I
bite I can be caught up in it for days, months, or even a lifetime. With
mindfulness, even if we get caught, there's no need to despair.
When we recognize that we're caught, it is much easier to remove ourselves from that experience than it is to remove a fish
from a hook. A large part of the battle is already won because
that recognition brings us closer to the present moment.

The present moment is the place where we can recognize: There is the content of experience; there is something
in the content that we find appealing—something that tempts
us to make it our own; and there is a desire compelling us to
grab onto that content. When we're connected to our present-
moment experience in this way, there is the wisdom that tells
us, *I know this process of content-appeal-desire-compulsion is not to*
be trusted. I am going to step back from that and let this more spacious
place of awareness and recognition establish itself. Then I can proceed
from that place, rather than from the place of compulsion.

So whenever we experience these empty times of waiting
for something to happen, we can use them as opportunities to
investigate and reflect on the content of consciousness. This is
hard work. It is the work of spiritual life and one of the main
activities we do with spiritual practice. It is not like having a
livelihood in which we are given a clear task, day after day—a
livelihood where we might have the attitude that, *As long as I do*
this I don't have to worry about anything. I just do my job, go home,
go to bed, and everything is okay. I don't have to give it much thought.
This is not how it is with spiritual life, nor with spiritual practice. We are not here merely to have a place to stay and food
to eat—that would be a terrible motivation. The motivation to

be here has to be for something noble, something that involves the dignity of work and the dignity of silence. Whenever we sit in silence, whether in this room or someplace else, it's not a time for mindless waiting. It's a time for work.

Solitude and Engagement

Luang Por Pasanno • May 2005

With Luang Por Sumedho visiting, this last week has been a full one, with lots of contact and engagement. That's the nature of monastic life; even though there's an underlying foundation of simplicity, one goes through various phases of solitude and group activity. It's important to make a conscious effort to bring things back to a life of more solitude and less engagement. It's interesting to see how the mind picks up a particular way of relating and then rolls along with it, so we need to make that conscious effort to pull back.

It's not as if engagement is bad—it's been a wonderful and fruitful time with Luang Por Sumedho here. But I think it's time to bring the mind back in and ask how we can integrate his inspiring presence into our lives. How do we actually live with awakened attention? How do we put our day-to-day lives on the line and make them examples of clear knowing, clear seeing? This is what he's talking about. To hear these words and then carry on with a scattered, miserable existence doesn't really cut it. How can we keep recollecting and applying these teachings, particularly in the next couple of days? We do our chores, we do our duties, and we do what needs to be done. But we should also try to give ourselves more time for solitude and let the teachings of Luang Por take root in the heart.

Death: A Cause for Brightness

Ajahn Amaro • November 2008

There is a skillful and beautiful Buddhist tradition for families and friends of someone who has passed away. The family members and friends come to the monastery and make offerings that support the monastic community. They receive *puñña*, merit from these offerings, and they dedicate that merit to the deceased, in whatever state of being he or she may have moved on to. In countries like Thailand, Sri Lanka, and for Buddhists who live in the West, there are certain occasions when family and friends come to make these offerings—some short period of time after the death, then perhaps six months after the death, and then the year anniversary of the person's passing away.

In the chanting that is done on those occasions, we don't recite verses like, "Don't worry, he's gone off to be with the angels forever. The Lord is looking after him, and he'll be happy up in heaven with the bunnies and the blackberries." Rather, we chant in a more reflective way in terms of the wholesome, unwholesome, and neutral dhammas, the internal and external dhammas, which comprise the different mind states and qualities of experience. Also, for those left behind, there are recollections such as, "All that arises passes away. Whatever comes into being disintegrates, and in its passing there is peace." They're not deliberately consoling on an emotional level, but very realistic: "Yes, life came to be, and now it's ended. It's dissolved." This acknowledges the sadness when someone close to us dies, without wallowing in that sadness. At the same time, we don't suppress it, trying to sugar over everything by thinking, *She's gone to a better place.* Well, maybe she has or maybe she hasn't.

In the Buddhist tradition there's a great deal of realism around the process of death, and it's important for us all to cultivate this quality of realism. What we know is that a life came into being, and now it's ended. That much we can be absolutely sure of. There's a natural feeling of loss and sadness, a sense that the person was around, a friend, close to us, but now gone. Even the Buddha experienced the loss of those close to him. There's a famous passage that takes place after the Buddha's two chief disciples, Sāriputta and Mahāmoggallāna, had passed away. The Buddha says to the gathered Saṅgha, "The assembly seems empty now that Sāriputta and Mahāmoggallāna are no longer here." So even a fully enlightened being like the Buddha can know and sense the loss of friends and companions. That's only natural and to be expected. It's realistic.

The customs of gathering together, taking precepts, making offerings, and dedicating the merit to benefit an individual are ways of taking that feeling of sadness and loss on the occasion of a person's death and uniting it with an act which is intrinsically wholesome, a brightening act of generosity and kindness. Acts of generosity and dedicating merit bring happiness, brightness, and invigoration to the mind and the heart. Over time, a succession of gatherings, making offerings, and creating wholesome kamma in relationship to that person slowly transforms the occasion of their death from being something associated with an experience of loss and absence into something that is much more a cause for brightness and happiness to arise.

Comfortable With Uncertainty

Luang Por Pasanno • June 2013

As we reflect on the traditional explanation of *anicca*—how things are impermanent, inconstant, always changing—it is especially useful to also reflect on anicca as a sense of uncertainty, or as Ajahn Chah would say, "It's not a sure thing." We tend to deny or gloss over the fact that we don't know things for sure. We feel uncomfortable with uncertainty or uncomfortable with not knowing something. It can be intimidating. But reflecting on anicca helps bring us back to the awareness of not knowing, of not being certain. We can be aware of the feeling that arises within us when we're in touch with that uncertainty.

When we are out of touch with our awareness of uncertainty, needless stress and suffering can occur. Take, for instance, the way it feels to express some view that we later learn is wrong. If we ask ourselves what it feels like when we express something that is wrong, we might say that it feels awful, embarrassing, or uncomfortable. But actually that is not really true. At the time that we're speaking, if we don't know that we are wrong and there's no way to discern that what we have said *is* wrong, then it feels just the same as when we are right, because at that point we think that we *are* correct and believe that what we have said is true.

As soon as we learn of our mistake, however, we likely will feel embarrassed—but only if, at the time we expressed our

200

view, we hadn't been open to the real possibility that our view might be wrong in the first place. In other words, if we have lost touch with the fact that, like all views and opinions, "It's not a sure thing," then we may likely feel ashamed or uncomfortable. But if we keep this notion of uncertainty with all that we do and say then when we do make a mistake—an honest mistake, based on some assumption rather than a deliberate lie—then it's not so much of a problem. It's uncertain, and we don't need to take it personally, thinking that *I'm such an awful person, I never get it right, I should have known better.* When we hold our thoughts and words with an understanding that anything we say could be incorrect, it tends to hurt a lot less. If we happen to be wrong, then we can shrug our shoulders and say to ourselves, *Oh, is that so? Okay, no problem.*

This is true with the way we relate to our moods as well. They're often screaming at us, *This is the way it really is!* To save ourselves the needless suffering that comes from believing and acting on our moods, we challenge them by reflecting, *Is this really true? Is it a sure thing that it is unchanging and permanent? Is it trustworthy?* Well, not for sure.

It's important to investigate and reflect on anicca—to take it in. When we do this, we're able to apply a true form of wisdom, which doesn't require knowing a lot of things. This wisdom is the ability to abide in a place of stability, even as we stay aware of and feel the uncertainty of things.

Beyond Determinations

Ajahn Yatiko • December 2012

If we wish to overcome obstacles in the heart to experience the transformation of the defilements, we need to recognize that it cannot be done through force. This is an important principle in our training. If we come across states of anger, irritation, or disappointment with ourselves or other people, and we're getting stuck in these states and dwelling on them, it doesn't work to simply make a determination to force ourselves to change them. We may think, *Okay, I'm going to try harder and make a new determination so I won't get stuck in these states.* That's not going to solve the problem.

Even so, when done properly, making a determination can be extremely valuable, and when a determination is valuable, if we slip up on it, then it's helpful for us to recommit to the determination straight away. But with deeply rooted internal states—such as irritation, ill will, being judgmental, and other defilements that linger within—we can't control our way out of them. We can't successfully determine, *I lost it, therefore, I'm going to try harder and not let it happen again.* Instead, it needs to come from a state of investigation and study. It doesn't help us or other people if we criticize ourselves for slipping up—and it also doesn't help to tell ourselves not to be critical.

We can't force ourselves to be happy, but there can be an investigation and a realization that we don't have to suffer over something. It really is possible to take a negative state, loosen it, and say to ourselves, *I don't have to suffer over this—it's really not necessary for me to suffer.* If that sort of loosening seems impossible, it merely means we haven't found the right entry point into the state we're working with. There *is* some entry point, some place where we're clinging and hanging onto negativity, and there *is* a way to let go of it. We have to know that, to have faith in that, and to trust in that. We can say to ourselves, *This is not who I am, and there is some way to let go of this. There's somewhere inside where I can loosen my grip. There has to be. If there weren't, that would be the end of this whole spiritual path.*

When these states arise, to a certain extent, determinations can be helpful to deal with them. But in order to fully uproot them, we have to use introspection, investigation, and self-study, reminding ourselves that we don't have to suffer over anything. If we can be clear on that, then we can even work on states that seem impossible to deal with, like physical agony—things that seem out of our control and things that really *are* out of our control. We can find a way to loosen our grip so we don't suffer. And that, of course, is the core of our practice.

A Mirror on Desire

Luang Por Pasanno • June 2005

Reflecting on the four requisites—clothing, food, shelter, and medicine—we can try to be more clear about what we need and what we merely want or desire. This can often become a bit cloudy in the mind. If we try to rely on what is truly necessary for a simple life, and question the desire or feeling of need that comes up, then things can become a bit clearer, and we are better able to understand how it is that desire keeps pushing us around.

Our lifestyle is so simple that the mind focuses on things very strongly and builds a case for what it thinks it really needs. But when we reflect, investigate, and question, we realize that it isn't actually a need at all—it's just another desire. So use the requisites as a means to understand the mind; use them as a mirror to see clearly what appears in the mind and what the mind is scrambling to get.

Having this prescribed lifestyle is very fruitful and encourages us to reflect more clearly about the nature of our desire and attachments. Being an alms mendicant with requisites and living in the monastery with this fundamental simplicity gives us a clear opportunity to unravel the way the mind complicates things, makes things problematic, and takes us away from fundamental contentment. The tools of our lifestyle are the Vinaya, the teachings, the requisites, our day-to-day activities, and the practice itself. We don't necessarily live by an extraordinary standard, but we use these tools that give us the opportunity to reflect, investigate, and learn to understand the mind in and of itself.

This Is Who I Am

Ajahn Karuṇadhammo • April 2013

Before the work meeting, a few of us were talking about different kinds of characteristics, traits, and qualities we each have and how easy it is to indulge in our personal attributes. Some people are good visualizers and can easily create certain kinds of images in their heads. Others can remember music. I was reflecting how easy it is to take those characteristics that are an integral part of each of us and pick them up in a way that makes us think that's who we are. Whether it's positive qualities or negative qualities, we come into the world with these attributes based on past actions and past habitual conditioning. Whatever they are, we easily identify with them and believe that's who we are: *I'm a person who has abilities in construction, carpentry, or computers. I'm a person who has a lot of anger, sensual desire, fear, or anxiety.* We take these different kinds of qualities we experience throughout our lives and personalize them, creating an image of ourselves in our own minds.

We do the same with other people. We see certain qualities, characteristics, or habits, so we identify a person as a particular type or someone who always has a certain characteristic. *He's an angry person. She's a person who has a lot of sensual desire.* Even if we're smart enough and know about Buddhist practice to the extent we don't really believe that's who we are, for the most part that's still how we operate. We continue to go through our daily activities, seeing the world of ourselves and the world outside through that perceptual lens of good and bad qualities. To counter this tendency, we persist in chipping away at that sense of solidity, that sense of a permanent self.

Every time we find ourselves lamenting over an unskillful quality or habit we have or puffing ourselves up thinking we're exceptionally good in some area, it's important to keep reflecting, *Well, that's not really who I am.* These are just qualities that come from conditioning—sometimes through skillful attention, sometimes through unskillful attention—and they're essentially a conglomeration of images and ideas that have formed into the perception: *This is who I am.* Try to see them objectively as conditioned qualities and don't take ownership. By recognizing this constant change and flow of characteristics moving through consciousness we can see clearly that we are merely holding onto shadows. We can learn not to hold onto these characteristics so tightly and watch them arise and cease, realizing their conditioned nature. If we can see little bits and pieces of how these different characteristics are dependently arising based on causes and conditions, then that strong and limiting sense of self starts to slowly disintegrate. Through this process we can understand that we aren't bound by the sense of *me, mine, myself*—the sense of entrapped solidity. It's good to bring this up as a recollection moving throughout the day, letting go little by little, and not feeling so entangled by our images and perceptions.

Being With Resistance

Ajahn Jotipālo • November 2012

In one of the Dhamma talks Ajahn Chandako gave recently, he said the best way that we, as monastics, can support people in the world, support ourselves, and support the people who support us, is to develop the monastery and develop our individual practices. We can do this by investigating our tendencies and mind states to see whether we are moving toward contentment and communal harmony or if we are moving toward a tendency to control—trying to push people around with our words or attitudes, or trying to manipulate conditions to meet our preferences. It's important to stop and ask ourselves, *What's the tendency there? What's the mental habit?*

As we all know, during these fifteen-minute morning work meetings, the work monk assigns a job to each of us. When I was a junior monk, I would feel a tense sense of resistance during the entire meeting because there were certain things I didn't like being asked to do. Years later, when I became the work monk, these tendencies weren't there at all because I had control. But even later, when it was again someone else who had the work monk job, my tendency toward resistance came back. This is only an example—a reminder that our tendencies to feel resistance, or any unwholesome tendencies, simply arise out of causes and conditions. It's important not to see them as wrong, but simply as tendencies of the mind.

With that understanding, we can investigate what is happening for us in the moment when resistance arises, and give ourselves space around the feeling that is present. We don't need to push these experiences away by bossing people around, trying to change things, or becoming reclusive. Rather, we can look at the feeling of resistance and learn how to *be* with it. We can observe how the feeling changes or investigate the fear that underlies resistance, breaking it all down. When we do this, it's possible to see that there's nothing worth fighting against—there's really nothing to be gained by being caught up in a mind state of resistance.

The Breath Through the Fog

Ajahn Yatiko • December 2012

Ajahn Chah said that when watching the breath, it's important to understand that our thinking doesn't have to stop. This is a very useful point. Often when we're watching the breath, we get lost in a train of thought and eventually remind ourselves to come back to the breath. In many guided meditations, we often hear the phrase, "Come back to the breath." We can start to feel that thinking is a problem, as if there is a battle between thinking and the breath. It can become unpleasant because we're fighting against our thinking. Rather than battling like that, we might instead imagine that our thoughts are like fog. We can be aware of the fog of thought, and when the breath becomes more prominent we can observe the breath.

Another way to look at it is that the breath is always there, waiting to be observed. We look through thoughts to *see* the breath like we look through a fog to see a light post or beacon. Rather than feeling we have to stop the thinking, we try to see through it. It's okay for thinking to be there if we have this attitude of trying to look through it. Observing in this way, we're not compelled to give thoughts a lot of attention; we're not interested in them. If we are able to observe our meditation experience from this point of view, it's easy to remember that our efforts in meditating aren't for the purpose of thinking, but rather that they're aimed at connecting with the breath. By having this attitude of looking through our thoughts, it can help us feel more harmonious toward them. By contrast, when thoughts arise, if we respond with, *Not again! I have to watch the breath,* then we have a sense of failing. This defeats our aim of cultivating ease and contentment.

In daily life as well, we often perceive thoughts as a problem we have to get rid of, and the same attitude can arise with the other experiences in our lives. We have certain emotions, moods, and interactions we want to get rid of because we perceive them as unhelpful, irritating, and annoying. We get into a battle between what we like and what we don't like. Instead, we can perceive experiences to be like fog. When we see them this way, there's nothing we have to suffer over. Ultimately, we will understand that there is no experience or feeling we have to hold onto or be afraid of in this world, in this life. If we have our hearts set on peace, truth, contentment, and virtue, then with that as a refuge, we don't have to fear anything. When we commit ourselves to these principles and values, everything we experience throughout the day is easier to let go of. We can see through it all.

Everything becomes transparent in the light of this attitude—at least it does when we can *access* that attitude. To do that, we have to put it into words we can repeat to ourselves so that we can come back to this perception of seeing through the fog of thought and experience. This can be as simple as telling ourselves, *What I am being distracted by is just thought or some other experience, nothing more, and it is okay for it to be here in my mind while I am following the breath.* This is the way the mind can settle and become clearer and more peaceful. We should try to see through everything in this way. When we do this with thoughts, they tend to subside. Thinking becomes less problematic—the breath becomes more evident. Clarity and peace arise.

Inner Stillness

Luang Por Pasanno • July 2005

As I was reading some teachings by Ajahn Munindo, a phrase he used resonated with me, and I find it useful to bring up and contemplate. He spoke of inner stillness—specifically, trying to attend to things such as performing one's duties or engaging with what needs to be done, with a quality of inner stillness.

Often the mind is impinged upon by the notion that it should be reacting, moving, or shifting. It's like the mind is waving its arms around trying to get attention: "Don't forget about me!" But if we return to inner stillness rather than going to the excitement, the movement, the reactions, and the ups and downs of the mind, then we can start to see arising and ceasing more clearly. We can recognize the pull of a particular impingement as simply something else that arises and ceases. This allows the mind to settle, which in turn fosters the quality of inner stillness even more.

Though our minds may come up with their justified indignations or justified attractions, if we hold these things within a framework of inner stillness, then we can make a choice to stop ourselves from being pulled in different directions. Instead, we can surround ourselves with this quality of inner stillness, and allow that to be what informs our practice and our engagement with the outer world.

Practicing in this way with our many duties can positively affect the experiences we have back in our dwelling places—

when sitting or walking in solitude—so that this alone time, too, can be imbued with the quality of inner stillness.

The Path of Non-Contention

Ajahn Amaro • September 2008

Often when we practice loving-kindness, *mettā*, it involves an active well-wishing to all beings, such as when we repeat the phrases, "May you be happy, may they be happy, may all beings be happy, healthy, safe, at ease," and so forth. Certainly that's an important part of loving-kindness meditation. But in a more essential, practical way, the quality of mettā is not only a well-wishing toward other beings; it also has to do with how we relate to our own mind states and the way we handle the different moods, feelings, and perceptions that arise within us. If we are repeating those mettā phrases and cultivating those sentiments toward external beings, yet internally relating to our own mind states in a semi-conscious or unconscious, reactive way, then all of those noble sentiments and qualities we direct outwards don't have much fuel, they don't have much of a foundation. To make the practices of mettā meditation really fruitful and genuinely relevant and effective, there needs to be both the external element and the internal element—relating with loving-kindness toward our own mind states, moods, bodies, thoughts, and feelings.

When there's an irritation, an impatience arising, a sense of things having shortcomings, or when we feel ourselves to be imperfect or not beautiful in some way, then it's easy for us to criticize and blame ourselves. We can quickly get upset with a mind that won't stop thinking or has stray thoughts and unwanted memories, ideas, fears, feelings, desires, and dislikes. Ajahn Sumedho addresses all these tendencies by expressing the essential attitude of loving-kindness as, "not dwelling in aversion." Rather than expecting to be affirmatively affectionate toward our bodies, thoughts, and feelings, it's merely a sense of not finding fault with them, not dwelling in aversion. That much is doable.

To establish the attitude of loving-kindness—the genuine heart of mettā—is to establish within ourselves a heart of non-contention, a heart that is accepting and accommodating of all mind states. This doesn't mean to say that we are approving of every thought we have, or that all our feelings of selfishness, violence, aggression, jealousy, and fear are beautiful, wonderful adornments for the world. We're not trying to pretend or allow ourselves to get lost in delusion, confusing the skillful and unskillful. Instead we're simply trying to recognize that everything belongs, whether it's a noble and wholesome thought, or a selfish, fearful, jealous, or greedy thought. They all belong. They're all attributes of nature. When we cultivate this quality of non-contention and acceptance toward all our inner qualities—feelings, thoughts, perceptions, memories, ideas, and fantasies—then the heart is not divided, and there's unity, a unification of the heart.

Without this fundamental unity of mettā in our hearts—this fundamental welcoming inclination and recognition that our internal attributes, good or bad, are all aspects of the natural order—it's impossible to have a genuine, substantial attitude of loving-kindness toward others, because the heart is divided.

So we can take some time to pursue and explore these themes and to reflect on them, seeing throughout the course of the day how often the mind wants to contend against our own bodies and their limitations, our feelings and thoughts, and the world around us. We can take it all so personally. While simply digging a hole in the ground we might think, *That rock is determined to get in my way!* But mettā is the heart of non-contention. We can learn how to work with the world so that regardless of how obstructive things may seem to be, how unwanted and unbidden, we can recognize that there's no need to start a fight or contend against the world—it's up to us.

When this recognition takes hold, we can see that there is always a path to working with the way things are, a path that leads us toward greater clarity and peacefulness, and all of this is based fully upon our cultivating an attitude of non-contention, of basic loving-kindness.

Becoming a Somebody
Forgetting About Everybody

Luang Por Pasanno • April 2013

As human beings, we each have a propensity for wanting to become a distinct *somebody*. This propensity shows itself almost constantly, both in formal practice and in our ordinary, day-to-day activities. It has to do with the hopeless search for worldly security and stability. Most people spend their whole lives on that search, but instead of finding security and stability, what they get is a sense of isolation—not really attuning to themselves or to the world around them. If we're not careful, this can be a danger for us here, as well.

A prime example is the way we relate to our assigned duties and chores. We become the somebody who manages the book distribution, or the somebody who looks after the computers, or the somebody who does the trash, or whatever. We hone in on the particular thing we're doing, and then conjure up a sense of ourselves as being the somebody who does that thing. Then it's easy to think: *Alright, I have my task. I don't have to do anything more than that. I don't have to be concerned anymore with what needs to be done outside of my job. I'm safe and secure; things are okay.*

That sort of thinking blocks us from developing mindfulness and attentiveness in huge areas of our lives—the world we're in and what's happening around us. Thinking like that can cause us to feel isolated. We set ourselves apart from the community, weakening our connection with all the other somebodies here who are doing other things that need to be done.

To avoid these dangers, rather than being somebodies who do only what we're assigned, we can instead be attentive to whatever might need doing. We can ask ourselves: *How can I help? How can I support the other people around me? What would be of service?* When everyone reflects in that way, and acts accordingly, the whole community can enjoy a sense of well-being and happiness, and we may personally learn that there's no real need to make ourselves into somebodies at all.

Reversing the Tendency to Decline

Ajahn Yatiko • May 2013

Last night a number of the monks had an opportunity to go up to Ajahn Dtun's *kuṭi* for a discussion on Dhamma. One of the themes brought up was the tendency for personal standards to decline in one's practice. This is an important trend to examine. We can look at the direction our practice has taken over time—how we started, how we've been practicing, and where our practice seems to be headed. That's something for us monastics to explore, because we can sometimes think of our practice as merely the form of being in robes. But actually, it's the heart that's practicing; the practice is not about taking on a role or simply putting on a robe. So we should ask ourselves, *Where is this leading, in the long run? What is the destination of the practice I'm doing now?*

There are two extremes for monastics that come to mind. One is moving toward the sense world, which strikes me as a nihilistic place with an emptiness to it. The other is moving toward some state of being—becoming a certain type of person, identifying with a role or believing that our goal is to become something different, improved, efficient, or whatever. These are the two extremes. So we can reflect on this and ask ourselves, *Is my practice moving in the direction of cessation and peace? Or is it moving toward the world of the senses or becoming?*

We can bring mindfulness and attention to this inquiry so as to see the direction of our practice. Once we see this direction clearly, we can reflect on what we need to adjust or correct. We do this so that our practice is moving in a more direct, straight, and less wavering direction toward a state of peace, understanding, and calm.

Facilitating Harmony

Luang Por Pasanno • October 2013

In several suttas, the Buddha points to *cāga* as a quality that facilitates harmony. *Cāga* is an interesting word. It means giving or sharing and also giving up. It's not only the quality of generosity, but also the ability to give up our fears, views, and opinions—things that end up creating moods and feelings of disharmony.

Another quality the Buddha points to that facilitates harmony is *piyavācā*—endearing, timely, and kindly speech. We use piyavācā in all our interactions, such as when we express our wishes, needs, and requests. With piyavācā, it is said, our speech will be "loved by many."

It can be a challenge to apply piyavācā when we're tired or when we're dealing with a lot of people at the same time. Cāga too, can be difficult, especially when we're feeling stressed or fearful. But they're both part of the training. We train to recognize when our speech isn't endearing or kind and then we reestablish our intention and start again. Likewise, we train to recognize our resistance to sharing or giving up and then make an effort to let go. By starting over with a new intention of cāga or piyavācā, we again place ourselves in a position of creating harmony.

Punching the Clock

Ajahn Karuṇadhammo • August 2013

It's easy to slip into a preprogrammed mode, flowing through the day on automatic pilot, especially when we're organizing our tasks for the day and engaging during the work period. Whether it's in the office, the kitchen, or out in the forest, we usually know what our tasks are and can click into autopilot mode quite easily. We can become completely absorbed in our activities—identified with them or with being the doer of particular tasks. This is when mindfulness, clear comprehension, attention, and alertness can all lapse.

The goal of the practice, and of the contemplative lifestyle in general, isn't simply to go to work in the morning, punch the time clock, and mentally check out. Nor is it helpful to take the view that when the work is out of the way, then it's time to practice. Instead, as much as possible, we are looking for a continuity of mindfulness and clarity throughout all of our activities, and that means bringing to mind a suitable object for focusing one's attention—that's what mindfulness is. We choose a wholesome object for this, one that will lead to skillful states of mind. Sometimes that's difficult, especially if we are doing work that requires us to be mentally focused. I think office work is among the most challenging in this regard, but it can be just as challenging out in the field if we find ourselves needing to think and plan for things. That's understandable and to be expected, but we try and attend to our duties with a sense of lightness and clarity. When tough moments arise, particularly if we are doing physical work, then we put effort into recollecting what we are doing in the moment. We can know our physical sensations clearly, and focus on something that will lead to a wholesome mind state, rather than a deluded one.

We keep the focus on the body, always here in the present moment. This is easier to do during physical work, as we can notice the very simple, basic, and uncomplicated position of our bodies and remain attentive to the movements as they occur. This is described in the Satipaṭṭhāna Sutta: knowing whether we are sitting, standing, walking, or lying down. Noticing the basic posture of our bodies is something we can do right now. As we walk, we can pay closer attention to whether we're looking forward, looking back, extending or contracting our arms. We can also see movement from one position to another, squatting, kneeling, hammering, typing on a computer, or even turning to answer the phone. It's simply a practice of giving attention to the basic movements of the body as a way of grounding oneself in mindfulness. This way of practicing has the potential to lead to a sense of settledness in the mind and the body. It helps keep us from becoming completely, 100 percent swept away with what we are doing, and allows us to maintain a bit of objectivity moment by moment. We do this by building up a momentum of pauses, stopping every now and again and feeling the presence of the body.

The Right Balance of Effort

Luang Por Pasanno • June 2005

Since today is a community work day, it's good to reflect a bit on effort. When we're working, how do we sustain our effort? How do we keep the kind of steadiness and pace that allows us to put forth effort without wearing ourselves out?

In meditation, we have a chance to notice how difficulties can arise when we're focused on trying to get or achieve something in our practice, when there's an agitated energy of doing. Or we can notice a holding back of effort and how the mind can sink with that. With these observations we better understand how effort works, and we can apply this understanding outside of meditation as well. When we're working or doing any kind of chore, it's helpful to consider how to apply effort so there's a steadiness, not a holding back or sinking, and not an agitated energy of doing.

We can also examine the way we limit ourselves through perceptions of what we think we can do. When we limit ourselves with perceptions, ideas, or fears, we're not able to put forth much effort. Contrary to these perceptions and fears, if our effort is balanced, then the more effort we put into something, the more energy we get back. There's a nice feedback loop of supporting energy that comes from putting forth the right kind of effort. When we learn to use effort in an appropriate way, we find ourselves buoyed up by the energy coming from that.

Being able to apply effort with steadiness and balance is an important skill. To develop this skill, we need to experiment with and look closely at how we apply effort and the results of applying effort. When we're able to apply ourselves in a steady, balanced way, we begin to get a feel for what the Buddha meant by "unremitting energy, unwavering effort." According to the Buddha, this factor of effort is crucial for liberation.

Cultivating Present-Moment Perception

Ajahn Yatiko • June 2012

When we think about something repeatedly, it tends to become a fixed perception for us, and we think about it even more. For example, if we have a work project and think about it throughout the day, we build up that perception of the project, and our tendency to think and proliferate around it becomes a world unto itself, a perceptual world we inhabit. This world-creating tendency builds momentum throughout the day, throughout the week. When we go up to our *kuṭis* in the afternoon and do sitting and walking meditation, these worlds we've created manifest themselves, and we think about them yet again.

But the corollary is also true. If we cultivate the perception of the present moment, that too will develop momentum. This does not mean, however, that cultivating this perception comes easily. When we get onto the walking path, for instance, there may be a tendency to think about computers, to think about a work project, or whatever. The untrained mind naturally wants to wander or obsess and proliferate—to disconnect from what is happening now. So we need to exercise discipline, saying to ourselves, *No, now is the time to be in the present moment.*

Sometimes getting the mind back on track simply requires us to relax our mental efforts. This can calm the mind so it's able to come back, seemingly of its own accord. Other times we need to exert a conscious effort to reconnect with the present. At first when we do that, we can only sustain the connection for a little while before losing it again. That's because it's a perception; left to its own devices, it comes and goes, like all other perceptions. If we want to sustain this present-moment perception, to develop a mastery around it, we have to cultivate the perception repeatedly, over and over again. When some little obstacle pushes us off in this direction or that direction, we do our best to find our way—to find a direction in which we can drop all obstacles and come back to the present.

Experiencing the present moment is always a relief and always refreshing. If we're not experiencing it that way, it's probably not the present moment! It's possible there's some residual attachment we're not seeing or acknowledging. So while it is true that cultivating a perception of the present moment is our duty, it is also true that fulfilling this duty is a most gratifying and uplifting experience. Remembering that point, we can undertake our duty with enthusiasm and a light heart.

As monastics living here at Abhayagiri, we have the opportunity and support to cultivate this present-moment perception. Such cultivation is vital—it's an invaluable tool for developing the mind and creating a foundation for deep insights into who we are, into the nature of this mind and body. Let us use this day for cultivating our perception of—and connection with—the present moment.

The Protective Power of Truth

Ajahn Jotipālo • November 2013

In quite a few of our *paritta* chants there is the line "*etena sacca vajjena sotthi te hotu sabbadā,*" which is roughly translated as, "by the utterance of this truth may there be safety, protection." About a month ago I was on my solo retreat reading a book about the stories behind the parittas, the protective chants. There was this touching tale from the Quail's Protection Chant for warding off fires. As the story goes, there is a baby quail that is alone in its nest out in a field and a fire begins to approach the nest. The quail is too young to take flight and not strong enough to get itself to the ground and run off. Its parents are out foraging for food. The baby quail is really in a desperate situation so it makes a statement of truth, which is, "I'm alone, without my parents, I'm weak, I can't fly or run away, and there is a huge fire approaching. By the utterance of this truth may I be protected" (Cp 79–82). In the story, the wind then shifts, and the baby quail is saved.

I was reflecting on this in terms of truth and honesty—really being present for what is happening as well as taking stock of the situation we're in. If there is some difficult interaction we have with someone, we can try to catch our reactions before getting upset or offended and try to relate to the truth of our experience. Sometimes when we state the simple truth to ourselves that, *This hurts,* we can cut it off right there. We don't have to go any further into the difficult situation. That's a good

thing, because if we did go into it further we'd likely compli-
cate the matter—*Why did this have to happen to me? It's not fair. I
didn't do anything to deserve this!*—and then get lost in negativity.
So instead of doing that, we can emulate the baby quail. Even if
the wind had not shifted and the quail had died, well at least he
wasn't blaming anyone, wallowing in self-pity, or being negative.

When Ajahn Sucitto was on pilgrimage in India, a group
of robbers attacked him and the layperson he was traveling with. In a book they later wrote together, Ajahn's traveling companion said of himself that during the robbery he re-
acted like an animal, fighting and fleeing out of fear. Ajahn
Sucitto just stayed there with the robbers, quietly and calmly
dealing with them. When the leader of the robbers held an
ax over Ajahn's head and was about to murder him, Ajahn
Sucitto calmly recited, *Namo tassa bhagavato arahato sammāsam-
buddhassa*, "Homage to the Blessed, Noble, and Perfectly Enlightened One." He came into the present moment, made an
honest assessment of the situation, and found himself truly
ready to die. Needless to say, Ajahn lived to tell the tale, and it
might well be that his honest presence and devotional recita-
tion on that day was what preserved his life.

There is a real protection and power which we receive
when, instead of focusing on what might happen in a negative
situation, we bring ourselves into the present moment, honestly and truthfully being available to the circumstances we
find ourselves in. There is no need to wait for fires or murder-
ous robbers to confront us—we can take advantage of this protective power in any moment of our day-to-day lives.

One-Pointedness of Mind

Luang Por Pasanno • June 2005

Yesterday, I listened to a talk by Ajahn Munindo. He spoke of a conversation he had with Luang Por Tate when Luang Por was about ninety-four years old. He asked Luang Por Tate, "What is the heart of Buddhism?" Luang Por answered simply, "One-pointedness of mind." That statement may be simple, but it has many implications. The quality of one-pointedness is needed to understand anything, to see and act clearly rather than getting swept up by reactions or habits. So we must try to focus and sustain one-pointedness by bringing attention back to what we are doing.

It's so easy to get distracted by what's going on around us externally, especially when doing chores or engaging with other people. Or, we can get distracted by the internal wanderings of the mind—thinking about how things could be or should be, or having reactions, worries, or doubts—proliferations in various shades and forms. We forget to establish a base of solidity—a foundation for the mind.

For that reason, we need to remember the importance of one-pointedness and to find skillful means to sustain it. In doing this, one-pointed mindfulness of the body can be an important anchor. That doesn't mean blocking out things around us, but rather, having a focal point. We maintain one-pointed attention, returning to the posture, physical sensations, movements, and touch. Whether we're going from here to there or standing in one place painting, we can bring attention to our body and cut through the mind's tendency to drift along.

If the mind is constantly drifting and dispersed, it will be unable to approach things in a clear fashion. But as we maintain one-pointed attention, a natural, energetic clarity arises. When it comes time to think, consider, and decide things, we will have the energy to do so. The mind will be clear and able to perform its task well.

Again, we need to cultivate one-pointedness as our foundation. This includes keeping precepts, composing the senses, and settling the mind, while reflecting and investigating with wisdom. We cultivate this foundation and let the practice grow from there.

What the Body Is Supposed to Do

Ajahn Karuṇadhammo • October 2013

I remember the first experiences Luang Por Liem had with his heart difficulties in Thailand. Apparently the condition had been going on for quite some time. He had symptoms of fatigue and probably shortness of breath, among other things. It wasn't until it was quite progressed that he did anything about it. When asked why it took him so long to look into it, his response was something like: "I thought this was what the body was supposed to do." That's the nature of the body, isn't it? Even if we do fix something in the body, something else is bound to eventually break.

All of the things that happen to us that we think shouldn't happen are simply reflective of the way *saṃsāra* is. It wouldn't be saṃsāra if things were always going perfectly. By the mere existence of saṃsāra we know that everything in the material world, the realm of the human body or psyche, is going to either break, change, or deteriorate according to certain laws of biology and kamma. These are natural laws that create the flow of arising and passing away. If we reflect, we can see how our expectations take us in a direction that sometimes leads to *dukkha*. For example, we get "the diagnosis" and we think, *Why me? I've done everything right. It's too soon. Why should this happen? Going to doctors and having treatments isn't what I was planning to do for the next few months or years!* We can feel extremely agitated and afraid in situations like this. Or maybe something in the material world breaks, and we really don't have time to deal with it—it feels frustrating. All of us experience these kinds of things, but we try to keep in mind and reflect that all of this—particularly the experience of old age, sickness, and death—is what we should expect to have happen. In fact, it's a miracle that it doesn't happen a lot sooner for most of us because this body is in a very fragile condition. Ajahn Chah is quoted as saying, "Everything we need to know can be learned from nature, if we just watch and pay attention." Whether it's in the material, physical, or mental realm, we can watch the nature of everything. We can see it arise, have its own life, change, and then pass away. That's the fundamental insight we need to have to truly understand saṃsāra and eventually realize complete liberation.

Bringing Sampajañña and Paññā to Work

Ajahn Amaro • August 2005

We have these community work days to create opportunities for the broader community to help contribute to the material fabric of the monastery and to support the life and energy of the Saṅgha. Along with emphasizing that, monasteries provide a context for individual spiritual development and cultivation. Our teacher Ajahn Chah strongly emphasized the essential quality of Saṅgha or community—learning how to collaborate and fit in with each other. So when we have these work days together, it is very much in the spirit of developing Saṅgha—cultivating a capacity to put forth effort and energy in a collaborative way. It requires a lot of attention to do it skillfully.

When we talk about *sati*, mindfulness, we often think about it in terms of being careful with the task or job we're doing. However, along with mindfulness, the other elements of clear comprehension, *sampajañña*, and wisdom, *paññā*, are crucial. Clear comprehension means that when we are engaged in an activity, we are at the same time aware of the context the activity takes place in. An example of this during the work period would be making sure the sharp end of the mattock we are swinging isn't about to go through the jaw of our work companion or making sure there isn't a soft fleshy object immediately behind us when we are turning around with a running chain saw in our hands. We want to avoid "The Redwood Valley Chainsaw Massacre," so we attend to our physical surroundings and also recognize that we are working with others.

Another quality we can be aware of is sharing. We are looking to do our part of the work and to include others as well. For example, sometimes we might become absorbed in a job that is really enjoyable, and so we completely forget or don't notice that there is another person in the group, standing there feeling like a spare part, waiting for us. Or we might do the opposite. It could be really hot outside, but other people seem to be enjoying the work, so we let them do it all while we sit and watch. With clear comprehension, we attend to the energetic feeling of the people we are working with. We pay attention to how we're feeling, how everyone else is faring, and we notice that if it's hot and dry, maybe the people working need a drink of water.

With *sati-sampajañña*, mindfulness combined with clear comprehension, there's an overall attending to and caring for not only our own needs, but the needs of the people around us. Our minds are attuned to making the time we spend working with others an opportunity to develop that collaborative spirit. It's not only an effort to benefit the monastery—creating more dwelling spaces, maintaining the finished buildings, digging a trench, clearing away brush, sorting out the stores, and so forth—it's also an effort to fit in and learn how to support others. It's about letting others support us as well, which can sometimes be more difficult than the other way around.

Another element we combine with sati is paññā, wisdom. Paññā is recognizing that all of this is impermanent, not-self, and unsatisfactory. So when we're putting something together or attending to some project, there's an overarching recognition that eventually it's all going to fall apart and disperse. There can be no inherent satisfaction in the projects we undertake if that satisfaction is based on a sense of permanence with these projects. With this insight into impermanence we can also recognize that these activities we are engaging in are not truly ours. This recognition brings a lightness to the tasks we engage in. When we are doing our work projects, we are developing expedient and useful skills but there's a relinquishing of what we do as well. There is no ownership or claiming of the things we bring into existence.

Another teaching that Ajahn Chah would stress over and over was to recognize that "the cup is already broken." The objects of the material world have within them *anicca*, an impermanent nature. They are destined to fall apart and disintegrate. The building we are currently constructing is already broken; it will fall apart or be demolished someday, so the efforts we're making are not toward a permanent end. We still continue to do what we do carefully, attentively, as well as we can, but there's a lightness, a spaciousness to the way it's held.

If we realize that the cup is already broken, then when the day comes that it does indeed break, our heart doesn't break with it. The cup physically smashes and we realize, *Oh, this is anicca. That's always been a part of it. Its anicca is simply ripening at this moment. Nothing has gone wrong; nothing bad has happened.* When we understand anicca, we are ready for the cup to break. There's no sense of loss or diminution in regard to its breaking.

When we hold things with wisdom in this way then there's a heedfulness, a fullness that we experience with every act we do. We're not trying to make it be more than it actually is, and we're not adding anything onto it. There's purity, simplicity, and a good-heartedness we can bring to everything we do.

The Dhamma of Contentment

Luang Por Pasanno • August 2012

Contentment is a good theme for all of us to consider. In doing so we want to learn how to be content with the circumstances around us, as well as with our own minds, internally.

Most of the agitation, negativity, and fault-finding that the mind cranks out is not so much about any big event that's happening outside. Almost invariably, it is a lack of internal contentment. When the mind is internally unable to find contentment, externally it finds something to be excited about, upset about, agitated about, or have an opinion about. It's usually really believable! We come up with the logic and all of the good reasons to justify our states of mind. There are plenty of good reasons if we look for them. But oftentimes, what's overlooked is the question, *Why can't I be content with this present moment, with this circumstance, with my mind and feelings as they are?*

This is a very important investigation. It's a fundamental basis for progress in practice. Until we learn how to direct our attention in that way, we're almost always driven by discontent and end up being caught up in some sort of sensual fantasy or internal rant or something that, at the very least, takes us out of the present moment. The challenge is to be able to draw attention to what's arising and investigate: *How can I be content with this present moment? How can I be content with myself?*

When the Buddha talked about being a refuge unto ourselves and taking Dhamma as a refuge, he didn't mean that we take refuge in the Dhamma of discontent. Our refuge is in the Dhamma of contentment, the ability to not be pulled away from the present moment. This is absolutely essential when we're talking about meditation—for the mind to become settled, peaceful, and still, we need to have the ability to be content with the breath or some other meditation object. In the suttas, the Buddha describes contentment as one of the characteristics of a great being or a noble one, an *ariya*. We learn to be content with our robes, alms food, lodging, and with our cultivation, our development of meditation.

This aspect of contentment is a fruitful area for investigation. We can experiment with it and find ways to draw our hearts closer to that quality.

The Trump Card

Ajahn Yatiko • October 2012

During the recent Western Monastic Conference, I raised a question with the Christian monks who were there, regarding an orthodox belief. I asked, "What happens to an unbaptized baby who dies in childbirth or an aborted fetus? Is it going to heaven or not?" One of the monks answered, "Well, technically it's not going to heaven, because it wasn't baptized." It's easy to think that's an outrageous belief. However, I like the way Brother Gregory explained the monk's answer. "Look at it this way: What trumps everything is that *God is just.* You can reduce everything to this one concept. Everything else fits into this understanding. If some issue doesn't fit, then either you're misunderstanding the issue, or it's been improperly communicated over time. *God is just,* so God is not going to send somebody to hell who doesn't deserve it." Fair enough. For Christians, maybe the ways of God are mysterious and beyond understanding, and the bottom line is *God is just.* That trumps everything.

Sometimes, over the many months and years of our Buddhist practice, doubts can creep in. In monastic life we have this form—the bowing, the routine, and the other structures we live within, and the doubt may arise, *Did the Buddha really teach all the rules we find in the Vinaya?* Or we may doubt whether certain parts of the early discourses are legitimate. *Did the Buddha really teach those suttas in the Dīgha Nikāya that seem so mythical?* How do we deal with that? In Buddhism we don't have this concept

241

of a permanent deity or a just God—we can't rely on that. But there's another trump card we can play: *The Buddha existed, and he was fully enlightened.* So I can reflect, *Perhaps whatever doubts I have arise because the form has been distorted over time or because I'm not understanding how to see through the particular issue at hand. But the bottom line is, the Buddha existed, and he was fully enlightened.* That's a powerful perception, and it's important that we do not let anything get in the way of that.

We can dwell on the things we don't like, the things we find frustrating—those things that create doubt—and we can even come up with persuasive reasons why something we doubt is, in fact, wrong. But the effect of dwelling and thinking like this is that the heart can become discontented. We needn't invite that sort of discontent when we can just as easily dwell on our trump card. *The Buddha existed, and he was fully enlightened.* When I bring up this perception, there's immediate joy and love and a recognition that this form, with all its imperfections, has a lineage that connects the Buddha with ourselves, right now. Through hundreds of generations, we're connected in a direct and tangible way to the living, breathing, walking Buddha—who existed and was fully enlightened. We can easily forget that, because it may seem so far removed from our ordinary, day-to-day experience. So we need to make an effort to bring this trump card into consciousness.

This can be especially useful any time we're having issues with monastic life or for laypeople who might be struggling with doubt or with their faith. It can also serve as a foundation for our meditation. If we feel dejected because our *samādhi* meditation isn't working, or whatever, we can return to this one idea: *The Buddha existed and was fully enlightened.* It is easily accessible to us and uplifting. As we return to this one idea, over and over again, we may well find that it trumps all our doubts and difficulties.

Embodying Experience

Luang Por Pasanno • April 2011

This morning I was recalling how James Joyce described one of his characters: "Mr. Duffy lived a short distance from his body." In Dhamma practice, we're learning how to inhabit our bodies and our experience of having a body. It's easy for us to become dissociated or distant. It's as if bodily experience becomes a projection of the mind, or we find ourselves treating the experience of having a body as if it were an abstract concept. This doesn't end up being very fruitful for us.

In his seminal discourse on mindfulness of breathing, the Buddha uses the verb *paṭisaṃvedeti*, which means "to fully experience." We fully experience the body as we breathe in and as we breathe out; we fully experience feelings as we breathe in and as we breathe out. It's a quality of inhabiting what is truly going on for us. If we stay even a slight distance from what we experience, then we don't see it clearly. And when we don't experience things clearly, we tend to create problems for ourselves.

That is why, when the Buddha taught the Four Noble Truths, he also taught a specific duty or response for each truth. He instructed that the First Noble Truth of *dukkha*—the experience of suffering, discontent, dissatisfaction, stress—is to be fully known. It's not until we fully know the experience of dukkha that we can begin to understand how we're contributing to it, how we're getting entangled in it, and how we're a part of its cause. The Second Truth—the cause of dukkha—is to be relinquished; the Third Truth—the cessation of dukkha—is to be realized; and the Fourth Truth—the path or practice leading to the cessation of dukkha—is to be developed. But it all begins with the First Truth: fully knowing.

Over and over again, the Buddha encourages us to develop our practice by fully engaging with and fully knowing what we encounter and experience. This is the very foundation on which the practice rests.

Practicing With the Five Hindrances

Ajahn Karuṇadhammo • December 2012

In our Dhamma practice, many of us will work with the five hindrances throughout the day—sensual desire, aversion, sloth and torpor, restlessness and worry, and doubt. It is helpful to pay attention to these hindrances and work with them because they are not only an obstruction when we sit in meditation, they're also concrete manifestations of the underlying tendencies: greed, hatred, and delusion. These are the tendencies that keep us moving through *saṃsāra*, cyclical rebirth. By examining the hindrances, we can see how these underlying tendencies manifest themselves in our daily lives. They tend to be more obvious to us if we are accustomed to them and start to work with them in a constructive way.

As Dhamma practitioners, we sometimes may think that our sole purpose is to be mindful of a particular state of mind that is occurring for us. This paradigm is correct in some ways, but not complete. We may think that if we're aware of being with a mind state then that alone is sufficient to deal with it. In other words, if we know that it's there, then presumably, we can watch its rising, its maintaining, and its cessation. This is a primary skill in our practice we need to develop: a straightforward, nonjudgmental awareness of a particular mind state.

However, there are also concrete and applicable antidotes we can use to work with the hindrances. In the Satipaṭṭhāna Sutta, the Buddha said that the five hindrances are to be known like all the other objects of mindfulness. In addition to knowing, we can reflect on how an unarisen hindrance arises, how we can deal with a hindrance that's already arisen, and how we can prevent its future arising. It's more than bare noting of a particular hindrance—we are learning more about it: how it comes to be, what encourages it, what nourishes it, and what denourishes it. We can understand how to work with it in a real, active sense when it's overwhelming and doesn't respond to bare attention.

It's a significant part of our practice to know how to recognize the hindrances. Although we probably have experienced most of them many times, we can have particular tendencies in regards to which ones we move to first. We might tend toward escaping from discomfort by using sensual gratification and indulgence. Or we may react to challenging situations with immediate irritation, by using a verbal retort, or with resistance, by having an internal sense of heating up. Likewise, we may become confused and doubtful, or shut everything out by annihilating ourselves with sleep, or worry and become restless and anxious.

We take note of where our buttons get pushed and the responses that tend to be most habitual, and start working with these aspects throughout the day. We do this to help prevent the hindrances from arising. One of the ways this is done is by working with a hindrance before it has arisen in the mind. For example, with aversion or irritation, we learn how to develop its antidote: loving-kindness. By developing loving-kindness, we are increasing its strength and availability so we can access it any time we need to use it.

As we become more familiar with our tool bag of antidotes, we weaken and diminish the power the hindrances have over us. We can therefore feel more confident and proficient in dealing with them so that we are not so easily blown off course.

The Khanti Pāramī

Luang Por Pasanno • April 2013

It is helpful to contemplate how to use *khanti*, patience, in our daily practice, and how we can cultivate it as a mental attitude during meditation. Patience is an underrated *pāramī* and considered in different ways, sometimes even misinterpreted. I remember Varapañño Bhikkhu disparaging himself, saying: "I just don't have any pāramīs of wisdom, meditation, loving-kindness, or anything like that. But at least I can just put up with this. I can build some khanti pāramī." His attitude reminded me of the depressed but lovable donkey Eeyore from *Winnie-the-Pooh*.

Khanti is actually a proactive engaging with experience in a way that's not getting caught up in, or swayed by, the reactions and impulses of either liking or disliking, or of desire and aversion. It has an enduring quality to it. One of the phrases the Buddha uses to describe the impulses of mind is *abhijjhā domanassa*, desire and aversion, or a gladness-sadness type of impulse. We can try to have an enduring and patient attitude toward that so we're not reactive. When we're not reactive, then desire and aversion, liking and disliking, go their natural way and cease. So when we're engaged in some sort of interaction, whether it's pleasant or unpleasant, the mind isn't getting swept up in it. Similarly, when we're engaged in some kind of task, chore, or duty, and we have been cultivating patience,

249

then what comes to mind is a kind of *gravitas*, a sense of weight, ballast, or anchor in the mind that isn't pulled around.

I've never come across a satisfying translation of khanti—"patient endurance" doesn't quite get it. In general, I think it's important to reflect on it in terms of how it manifests for us: *How do I turn the mind toward a quality that isn't swayed, pushed, or pulled?* It's a willingness to be present with experience and especially important in meditation. When any of the five hindrances come up, they feel quite compelling and true as moods. We attempt to have an enduring quality of mind that is present with the hindrances and attends to them as they follow their natural cycle: arising, persisting, and ceasing. They come into being and pass away. One of the functions of patience is to help us refrain from feeding our defilements. When we're not feeding or nourishing our reactive moods, then there's a real steadiness there. With khanti present, we're not trying to manipulate conditions around us so that they suit our preferences or to manipulate people to make them pleasing to be around. Neither worldly conditions nor people are going to fulfill our preferences or desires. But when we have khanti to receive our experiences, then we're not shaken by them.

As part of the ethos and flavor of Ajahn Chah's training, the development of the khanti pāramī was strongly encouraged so we would have a good, solid foundation in our practice—a foundation that helped to steady us despite the changing circumstances and conditions of our lives.

Reestablishing What Is Foundational

Ajahn Yatiko • May 2013

Our lives are uncertain in so many different ways. All sorts of curveballs could be thrown at us at any time, disrupting our flow. If we understand this, knowing curveballs happen, we don't have to see them as problems. Any anxiety we have around the future is not to be denied as part of our experience. We can hold it, be with it, and try to act responsibly toward it. At the same time, we can have mindfulness and see anxiety as simply a phenomenon, a perception arising in the present moment. If we closely examine whatever it is we're worried about, thinking about, or attached to, we see that very often it's nothing but an idea in our heads, and from that idea we can create a whole world of suffering. To penetrate and see this is an essential part of our practice.

We do need to take care of practical things, such as our tasks during the work period that starts a short while from now. But when we go out to do some work it is crucial that we do not set aside the insights we have realized—these can be understandings about the insubstantial nature of ideas and concepts, the past and the future, and their potential for causing us suffering. These insights are accessible and not that difficult to penetrate, but it takes determination.

We have to go into the stream of the compulsive mind that's going in a particular direction, very often the direction of *bhavataṇhā*. Bhavataṇhā is the ongoing creation of, and belief in, a solid and substantial self or identity that we are constantly propping up with roles, habits, ideas, views, and opinions—*I'm like this, I'm not like that.* We need to go against that bhavataṇhā, putting an anchor down in the stream of becoming. Penetrating through the illusion of bhavataṇhā is one of the most important aspects of our practice. It's more important than any of the little hobbies we have, the habits we've developed, the various ways we spend our time. We have to make sure that in our monastic lives we don't let the hobbies become foundational. If they do become foundational, then what *should* be foundational—meditation—simply becomes a pastime. When that happens it's tragic, and we need to do our utmost to cut it off.

To cut it off requires being aware of it. In the Anangaṇa Sutta—Without Blemishes—the Buddha points to the case where a person with a blemish "understands as it actually is, 'I have a blemish in myself.'" He has a blemish and *knows* he has a blemish, and therefore can be expected to exert himself to abandon that blemish. But a person who doesn't realize he has a blemish is not likely to do anything about it. So this is the starting point—being able to recognize a defilement as a defilement, being able to call it that. That's step one. Step two is to work with it.

Striking at the Heart of Renunciation

Luang Por Pasanno • May 2013

One of the teachings Ajahn Chah emphasized most consistently was on the theme of uncertainty—that everything is not for sure. In a monastery, for instance, it's common for the number of visitors to increase, like today, and then decrease; they're here for a while, then they disappear. This creates a constant sense of circumstances being uncertain, always changing.

We tend to conceive of our practice and training as being under conditions over which we have some control. We can take this opportunity today to investigate and reflect upon how we deal with our practice when it becomes apparent that conditions are really not under our control, when the monastery becomes an open house for more activity and people.

When circumstances change in a way we like, we tend to get excited and happy; when they change in a way that we don't like, we may get upset and irritable. In both cases, we're being swayed by the circumstances around us, and that's a shaky foundation on which to build our practice. So how can we stay present with what's happening without getting lost in the changing circumstances? The way to do that is through the quality of our attention—how we direct our attention, how clear we are, and how mindful we are. But mindfulness isn't always going to be present. For this reason, establishing an internal quality of renunciation is quintessential for us as practitioners.

The rules and conditions that are part of living in a monastery create a framework of external renunciation, such as the giving up of material things. That framework is in place to support an *internal* quality of renunciation, which needs to be cultivated at all times. Internal renunciation means we're not desperately holding on to circumstances, moods, and feelings. Giving up material things is not that difficult. When we give up our moods, views, opinions, and preferences, we are striking more at the heart of renunciation.

We learn to bring this quality of renunciation into our daily lives and interactions with others so that when circumstances change, we can let go and adapt to them. Today, for example, there's a large group of people visiting and things are happening all around us. If we try to control the situation—try to make things happen the way we want—we're likely to create problems. But everything will run smoothly if we turn to this internal quality of renunciation, doing our best by letting go of our moods, views, and preferences.

Full Awakened Awareness

Ajahn Amaro • October 2006

When there is full, awakened awareness, there is no identification with the body or with conditioned factors of mind. The realization of Dhamma is so complete that the life or death of the body is of as little consequence as the turning of the Earth is to the Sun. The body and mind are not-self, as is reiterated so often in the Buddhist scriptures, so the heart remains serene with all of life's ups and downs, its many psychological births and deaths, triumphs and failures, as well as the "big death" of the body's ending. As St. Theresa of Avila put it when expounding on this same theme, "We die before we die so that when we die we don't die."

Glossary

ajahn (Thai): Literally, "teacher." From the Pāli word ācariya; often used in monasteries as a title for senior monks or nuns who have been ordained for ten years or more.

anagārika: Literally, "homeless one." An eight-precept male postulant who often lives with bhikkhus and, in addition to his own meditation practice, also helps with certain services that are forbidden for bhikkhus to do, such as, using money, cutting plants, or cooking food.

anattā: Not-self, ownerless, impersonal.

anicca: Impermanent, inconstant, unsteady. Ajahn Chah often translated it as "not sure."

asubha: Unattractive, not-beautiful. The Buddha recommended contemplation of this aspect of the body as an antidote to desire, lust, and complacency.

bhikkhu: A Buddhist monk; a man who has given up the householder's life to join the monastic Saṅgha. He follows the Dhamma-Vinaya (the doctrine and discipline), the teachings of the Buddha as well as the Buddha's established code of conduct.

brahmavihāra: The four sublime or divine abodes that are attained through the development of mettā, karuṇā, muditā, and upekkhā (boundless loving-kindness, compassion, sympathetic joy, and equanimity).

Buddha: The historical religious leader and teacher who lived around 2500 BCE in the Ganges Valley of India. After his enlightenment, he established a monks', nuns', and lay community under the instruction of what he called the Dhamma-Vinaya—the doctrine and discipline. The word Buddha literally means "awakened one" or "enlightened one."

defilements: Impurities, vices. Unwholesome mental tendencies or inclinations that cloud the mind. In their most basic forms they are greed, hatred, and delusion.

Dhamma (Sanskrit: Dharma): In general, a spiritual or philosophical teaching describing the natural state of reality. When used in this book, Dhamma specifically refers to the teachings of the Buddha: a systematic understanding of suffering, its cause, and how one applies oneself to eliminate this suffering, thus ending the cycle of rebirth.

dhamma: Used as a term to define natural phenomena of the world, including phenomena of the mind.

dukkha: "Hard to bear," unsatisfactoriness, suffering, stress.

Eightfold Path: See Noble Eightfold Path.

Forest Tradition: The tradition of Buddhist monks and nuns who have primarily dwelled in forests emphasizing formal meditation practice and following the Buddha's monastic code of conduct (Vinaya).

Four Noble Truths: The first and central teaching of the Buddha about dukkha, its origin, cessation, and the path leading toward its cessation. Complete understanding of the Four Noble Truths is equivalent to the realization of Nibbāna.

kamma (Sanskrit: karma): Volitional action by means of body, speech, or mind. Kamma always leads to an effect (kamma-vipāka).

khandhas (Sanskrit: skandha): Heap, group, aggregate. Physical and mental components of the personality and of sensory experience in general. The five bases of clinging: form, feeling, perception, mental formations, and consciousness.

kuṭi: A small dwelling place for a Buddhist monastic; a hut.

Luang Por (Thai): Venerable Father, Respected Father; a friendly and reverential term of address used for elderly monks.

Māra: Evil, craving, and death personified as a deity, but also used as a representation of these elements within the mind.

mettā: Loving-kindness, goodwill, friendliness. One of the four brahmavihāras or sublime abodes.

Middle Way: The path the Buddha taught between the extremes of asceticism and sensual pleasure.

mindfulness: See sati.

Nibbāna (Sanskrit: Nirvāṇa): Final liberation from all suffering, the goal of Buddhist practice. The liberation of the mind from the mental effluents, defilements, the round of rebirth, and from all that can be described or defined. As this term also denotes the extinguishing of a fire, it carries the connotations of stilling, cooling, and peace.

Noble Eightfold Path: Eight factors of spiritual practice leading to the cessation of suffering: right view, right intention, right speech, right action, right livelihood, right effort, right mindfulness, and right concentration.

noble silence: Taking on the practice to only speak when necessary.

Pāli: An ancient Indian language related to Sanskrit. The teachings of the Theravada school of Buddhism were transmitted orally in Pāli for hundreds of years before being written down at the beginning of the Common Era in Sri Lanka.

Pāli Canon: The standardized collection of Theravada Buddhist suttas written in the Pāli language.

paññā: Wisdom, discernment, insight, intelligence, common sense, ingenuity. One of the ten perfections.

pāramī (Sanskrit: pāramitā): Perfection of the character. A group of ten qualities developed over many lifetimes: generosity, virtue, renunciation, discernment, energy/persistence, patience or forbearance, truthfulness, determination, goodwill, and equanimity.

paritta: Literally, "protection." Auspicious blessing and protective chants typically recited by monastics and sometimes lay followers as well.

pūjā: Literally, "offering." Chanting in various languages typically recited in the morning and evening by monastic and lay followers of a particular teacher, in this case the Buddha. Typically these recitations pay homage to the Buddha, Dhamma, and Saṅgha.

Rains Retreat (Vassa): The traditional time of year that monks and nuns determine to stay in one location for three months.

Some monastics will take this time to intensify their formal or allowable ascetic practices. Monks and nuns will refer to themselves as having a certain number of Rains Retreats which signifies how many years they have been in robes.

right action: One factor of the Eightfold Path which prescribes that one refrain from taking life, stealing, and sexual misconduct. In a broader context it can be understood as refraining from unskillful actions and encouraging skillful ones.

right effort: One factor of the Eightfold Path which describes how a practitioner endeavors to prevent or abandon unwholesome qualities as well as maintain and develop wholesome qualities within the mind.

right speech: One factor of the Eightfold Path describing the proper use of speech: refraining from lying, divisive speech, abusive speech, and idle chatter.

samādhi: Concentration, one-pointedness of mind, mental stability. A state of concentrated calm resulting from meditation practice.

Samaṇa: Contemplative or wandering ascetic. A samaṇa is literally a person who abandons the conventional obligations of social life in order to find a way of life more "in tune" (sama) with the ways of nature.

sampajañña: Clear comprehension, self-awareness, self-recollection, alertness.

saṃsāra: Literally, "perpetual wandering." The cyclical wheel of existence. The continuous process of being born, growing old, suffering and dying again and again, the world of all conditioned phenomena, mental and material.

Saṅgha: This term is used to conventionally describe the community of ordained monks and nuns practicing the teachings of the Buddha. However, from a noble or ideal view, it specifically describes the followers of the Buddha, lay or ordained, who have realized one of the four levels of awakening: stream-entry, once-returning, non-returning, or Nibbāna.

sati: Mindfulness, self-collectedness, recollection, bringing to mind. In some contexts, the word sati when used alone refers to clear-comprehension (sampajañña) as well.

sīla: Virtue, morality. The quality of ethical and moral purity that prevents one from engaging in unskillful actions. Also, the training precepts that restrain one from performing unskillful actions.

five spiritual faculties (pañc'indriya): Faith, energy, mindfulness, concentration, and wisdom.

sutta (Sanskrit: sūtra): Literally, "thread." A discourse or sermon by the Buddha or his contemporary disciples. After the Buddha's death the suttas were passed down in the Pāli language according to a well established oral tradition and finally committed to written form in Sri Lanka just around the turn of the common era. The Pāli suttas are widely regarded as one of the earliest records of the Buddha's teachings.

Triple Gem: The Threefold Refuge: the Buddha, Dhamma, and Saṅgha.

Upāsikā Day: A day for Abhayagiri lay devotees to visit the monastery and partake in an afternoon teaching.

Vinaya: The Buddhist monastic discipline or code of conduct. The literal meaning of Vinaya is "leading out," because maintenance of these rules leads out of unskillful states of mind. The Vinaya rules and traditions define every aspect of the bhikkhus' and bhikkhunīs' way of life.

wat (Thai): A monastery.

Oppty to dev. Mindfulness p70
Use activity to cultivate P2
foundation: awareness of
Body + feeling
Comfort + end of suffering p75
stretch ourselves, but Stay in
middle way. Search: what it is
that undermines tendencies
toward greed, hatred, delusion.
what are underlying roots of delusion

abhayagiri is complete p 77
"finish it everyday"
Every moment dharma
is complete

Cows in pasture p81
(Lord is my shepherd)
Clean Kuti, Clean mind 85 ①
Pain - stay w/it - review life:
my Life is good ② see me from
above, observe my body + mind

Caga giving over, relinquish 89
Operate in a community w/ certain
protocols - I give up "MY" way for
community way.
my Teacher "a mango Tree" p90
Full tree gets abused. ½ empty tree
no → simplify life, get spiritual
struggle we don't have to → peace +
tranquility? not always, Hints: .....
meditation ?

Wholesome action + recollection p23

Reframe (determined to suffer p31

{ Wholesome + bright states of mind,
  mind settles down "Contain the chicken" p33

faith + wisdom p 37

p39 Mindfulness of <u>death</u>: body
ckin in present moment, position,
posture, how moving thru space
mood?

<u>Death</u> vs <u>Wakefulness</u> p45

<u>Hatred</u> <u>does</u> <u>not cease</u> by
hatred <u>but</u> <u>by</u> <u>love alone</u>.

non-contention p 45

<u>Letting go</u> p 49 <u>fears, fixed views,</u>
<u>attachment + desires</u>

Intruding sense of suffering p 51
(attachmt = clear seeing)

Patience: Turning inward, p.53
turn toward the dukkha (pain)
I will be w/this situation.

impact right speech p 57

Generosity of respect p59
respect their highest motivation
<u>do good, do wholesome.</u>

Papañca Mill = mind incessant chatter
p 60

Present moment p. 63

67 (1) Goodness of others gratitude counteract
negativity, critical mind

(2) Temp short term solutions may be
counter productive in long run.